More great Puzzle Books at www.puzzlejuice.com

ABOUT THIS QUIZ

WELCOME TO THE ULTIMATE POPULAR MUSIC QUIZ BOOK. A QUIZ THAT TAKES YOU ON AN EXCITING JOURNEY THROUGH MODERN POP MUSIC HISTORY, FROM THE BIRTH OF ROCK N' ROLL IN **1954** ALL THE WAY THROUGH TO **2020** - FROM ELVIS PRESLEY AND CHUCK BERRY TO BILLIE EILISH AND DUA LIPA!

A QUIZ TO BRING ALL THE FAMILY TOGETHER! IF YOU LOVE POP MUSIC THEN CHILDREN, PARENTS AND GRANDPARENTS (AND EVEN GREAT-GRANDPARENTS!) CAN ALL JOIN IN THE CHALLENGE TO COMPLETE THE QUIZ.

THIS IS A HARD AND CHALLENGING QUIZ THAT'S SURE TO CREATE A LOT OF DEBATE AND DISCUSSIONS TO REACH THE CORRECT ANSWERS! LUCKILY, ALL THE ANSWERS ARE IN THE BACK OF THE BOOK, BUT THERE'RE NO MULTIPLE CHOICE QUESTIONS, YOU NEED TO KNOW YOUR STUFF OR KNOW SOMEONE WHO CAN HELP!

FULL OF POP MUSIC TRIVIA, YOU'RE ALSO SURE TO LEARN MANY NEW POP MUSIC FACTS TO AMAZE YOUR FRIENDS AND FAMILY!

THE USA AND UK HAVE LEAD THE WORLD IN POPULAR MUSIC FOR OVER SIX DECADES, SO THE MAJORITY OF THE QUESTIONS ARE BASED ON THOSE COUNTRIES, BUT THERE ARE ALSO QUESTIONS ABOUT ARTISTS AND SONGS FROM MANY COUNTRIES IN THE WORLD IF THEY'VE HAD SUCCESS IN THE USA OR UK, MAKING THIS A GLOBAL POP MUSIC QUIZ BOOK!

100'S OF QUESTIONS IN MULTIPLE GENRES OF POP MUSIC ARE COVERED IN THE QUIZ, IF YOUR FAVORITE MUSIC GENRE IS MISSING, WE APOLOGIZE! BUT YOU'LL STILL FIND, POP, ROCK, METAL, PUNK, RAP, HIP HOP, SOUL, R&B AND MUCH MUCH MORE!

ALL SORTS OF QUESTIONS ARE COVERED - NUMBER ONE SINGLES, BEST SELLING ALBUMS, DEBUT RELEASES, STAGE NAMES, BIRTHS, DEATHS, EUROVISION WINNERS, AWARDS WINNERS, MUSIC PIONEERS, GROUPS FORMING, GROUPS BREAKING UP, MAJOR MUSIC EVENTS AND LOTS MORE!

ALL THE QUESTIONS ON A SINGLE PAGE REPRESENT A SINGLE YEAR. ANSWER THE QUESTIONS ON A PAGE, THEN GUESS WHICH YEAR IT IS. SET YOUR OWN SCORING SYSTEM. A POINT FOR EACH QUESTION AND A BONUS POINT FOR THE YEAR IS A SIMPLE OPTION, BUT IT'S UP TO YOU.

A SINGLE YEAR HAS TWO PAGES INCLUDED SOMEWHERE IN THE BOOK. REFERRING BACK, OR FORWARD, IN THE BOOK MAY HELP TO ANSWER QUESTIONS OR FIGURE OUT YEARS.

SOME POPULAR ARTISTS SET RECORDS OR MAKE HEADLINES OR HAVE MASSIVE SUCCESS IN MULTIPLE YEARS, SO THEY WILL OFTEN APPEAR MORE THAN ONCE IN THE QUIZ.

GOOD LUCK!

THIS YEAR, KENDRICK LAMAR WON THE "PULITZER PRIZE FOR MUSIC" FOR WHICH LP, BECOMING THE 1ST NON-JAZZ OR CLASSICAL ARTIST TO WIN IT?

WHICH BAND IN THIS YEAR WON KERRANG'S "HEAVY METAL WORLD CUP" FOR THE SECOND TIME?

WHICH MULTI-INSTRUMENTALIST SINGER SONGWRITER WON SEASON 16 OF "AMERICAN IDOL" IN THIS YEAR?

DRAKE HAD THE MOST SUCCESSFUL SINGLE ON THE BILLBOARD HOT 100 IN THIS YEAR. WHAT WAS IT CALLED?

MULTIPLE AWARD NOMINATIONS AND CHART SUCCESS MARKED RAPPER POST MALONE'S 2ND STUDIO LP RELEASED THIS YEAR. WHAT WAS IT CALLED?

NAME THE YEAR:

IN THIS YEAR, THE EUROVISION SONG CONTEST IS WON BY THE UK FOR THE FIRST TIME. NAME THE SINGER AND SONG.

IN THIS YEAR, WHICH MONKEES SINGLE TITLE WAS CENSORED IN THE UK AND CHANGED TO "ALTERNATE TITLE"?

THE WORLD'S FIRST LARGE SCALE OUTDOOR ROCK MUSIC FESTIVAL WAS HELD IN CALIFORNIA IN THIS YEAR. WHAT WAS IT CALLED?

EDGAR FROESE FOUNDED WHICH BAND IN WEST BERLIN IN THIS YEAR?

"54-46 THAT'S MY NUMBER" WAS ONE OF THE FIRST REGGAE SONGS TO GAIN INTERNATIONAL POPULARITY. WHO SANG IT?

NAME THE YEAR:

2

THE BEST SELLING ALBUM OF THIS YEAR WAS TITLED "TRUE BLUE". WHO RECORDED IT?

THE FIRST ISSUE OF THIS UK MUSIC MAGAZINE WAS IN THIS YEAR. THE LAST ISSUE WAS IN JULY 2020. WHAT WAS IT'S NAME?

JORDAN, JONATHAN, JOEY, DONNIE AND DANNY RELEASED THEIR DEBUT ALBUM IN THIS YEAR. WHAT ARE THEY BETTER KNOWN AS?

THE WORLD'S BEST SELLING SINGLE IN THIS YEAR WAS BY "FALCO". NAME THE SONG.

STEFANI JOANNE ANGELINA GERMANOTTA WAS BORN IN THIS YEAR. WHO'S SHE BETTER KNOWN AS?

NAME THE YEAR:

3

IN THIS YEAR, WHY WAS ELTON JOHN FORCED TO END A CONCERT IN MELBOURNE, AUSTRALIA AFTER JUST 30 MINUTES?

WHO'S DEBUT ALBUM WENT STRAIGHT TO NO.1 IN THE UK IN THIS YEAR AND HELPED EVOLVE "BRITPOP" INTO A MUSICAL MOVEMENT?

IN THIS YEAR, WHICH UK ALT ROCK BAND RELEASED THEIR DEBUT ALBUM, "A STORM IN HEAVEN"?

WHICH ACTOR, AND SINGER IN THE BAND ALEKA'S ATTIC, TRAGICALLY DIED IN THIS YEAR?

IN THIS YEAR, WU-TANG CLAN RELEASED WHICH DEBUT ALBUM, NOW WIDELY REGARDED AS ONE OF THE GREATEST HIP HOP ALBUMS OF ALL TIME?

NAME THE YEAR:

WHICH "WALL OF SOUND" PRODUCER BEGINS HIS RECORDING CAREER IN THIS YEAR?

PERRY COMO SPENT 8 WEEKS AT THE TOP OF THE UK CHARTS IN THIS YEAR WITH WHICH SONG?

WHAT WAS BANNED BY THE IRANIAN GOVERNMENT IN THIS YEAR AS "A HEALTH HAZARD"

WHO SANG IN THIS YEAR "IT'S ONLY MAKE BELIEVE"?

WHO IS THE KEYBOARD PLAYER WITH THE BAND "SQUEEZE" WHO WAS BORN IN THIS YEAR?

NAME THE YEAR:

THEIR NAME COMES FROM A KIND OF BEEHIVE HAIRDO. WHICH US NEW WAVE BAND PLAYED THEIR 1ST GIG IN THIS YEAR?

WHICH SEMINAL UK PUNK ROCK BAND RELEASED THEIR DEBUT ALBUM - "RATTUS NORVEGICUS" IN THIS YEAR?

WHICH UK GLAM ROCK ARTIST TRAGICALLY DIED AS A PASSENGER IN A CAR ACCIDENT IN BARNES, LONDON IN THIS YEAR?

STUART GODDARD WAS THE LEAD SINGER OF WHICH BAND THAT FORMED IN THIS YEAR?

AN IRISH ROCK BAND NAMED "HIGHWAY STAR" FORMED IN THIS YEAR. THEY EVOLVED INTO A PUNK BAND AND CHANGED THEIR NAME TO WHAT?

NAME THE YEAR:

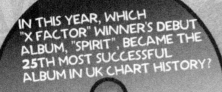

IN THIS YEAR, WHICH "X FACTOR" WINNER'S DEBUT ALBUM, "SPIRIT", BECAME THE 25TH MOST SUCCESSFUL ALBUM IN UK CHART HISTORY?

THE BEST SELLING ALBUM IN THE US IN THIS YEAR WAS "THA CARTER III" WHO WAS THE ARTIST?

EARNING $408M, THIS MADONNA TOUR BECAME THE HIGHEST GROSSING TOUR FOR A FEMALE ARTIST IN HISTORY. WHAT WAS IT'S NAME?

IN THIS YEAR, LADONNA ADRIAN GAINES RELEASED HER 1ST STUDIO ALBUM SINCE 1991. HOW IS SHE BETTER KNOWN?

THE WORLD'S BEST SELLING ALBUM OF THIS YEAR WAS "VIVA LA VIDA OR DEATH AND ALL HIS FRIENDS", BY WHO?

NAME THE YEAR:

ROCK AROUND THE CLOCK FIRST APPEARED IN THE BRITISH CHARTS IN THIS YEAR. WHO SANG IT?

WHO BECAME ELVIS PRESLEY'S MANAGER IN THIS YEAR?

WHO WROTE THEIR FIRST SONG TOGETHER "THE GIRL FOR ME" IN THIS YEAR?

CHUCK BERRY RECORDS HIS FIRST SINGLE, FOR CHESS RECORDS, IN THIS YEAR. NAME THE SINGLE.

"AIN'T THAT A SHAME" WAS RELEASED IN THIS YEAR AND REACHED NUMBER ONE IN THE US R&B CHART. WHO SANG IT?

NAME THE YEAR:

8

IN THIS YEAR, CAPTAIN SIR TOM MOORE BECAME THE OLDEST PERSON TO EVER TOP THE UK SINGLES CHART. HOW OLD WAS HE?

THE UK'S BEST SELLING ALBUM OF THIS YEAR WAS BY LADY GAGA. WHAT IS IT CALLED?

"FUTURE NOSTALGIA" LP REACHED THE TOP 10 IN 31 COUNTRIES AND NO.1 IN 13 COUNTRIES INCLUDING UK IN THIS YEAR. WHO IS THE ARTIST?

BILLIE EILISH AND WHO? WON THE MOST GRAMMY'S AT THIS YEAR'S GRAMMY AWARDS.

IN THIS YEAR, LEAD VOCALIST OF INDUSTRIAL MUSIC PIONEERS, THROBBING GRISTLE SADLY DIED. WHAT WAS THIS PERSON'S NAME?

NAME THE YEAR:

THIS YEAR MARKED THE 75TH ANNIVERSARY OF THE BIRTH OF WHICH ROCK N' ROLL ICON?

IN THIS YEAR, WHICH CHARITY ALBUM BECAME THE FIRST DIGITAL-ONLY ALBUM TO TOP BILLBOARD **200** ALBUMS CHART?

WHICH UK BRITPOP BAND, FRONTED BY GAZ COOMBES, SPLIT UP IN THIS YEAR, BEFORE REFORMING IN **2019**?

THIS YEAR'S UK GLASTONBURY FESTIVAL WAS HEADLINED BY STEVLAND HARDAWAY MORRIS. WHO'S HE BETTER KNOWN AS?

LADY GAGA BECAME THE 1ST ARTIST IN HISTORY TO HAVE HER FIRST **6** SONGS ALL REACH NO.**1** ON BILLBOARD POP SONGS CHART. NAME THE **6**TH SONG.

NAME THE YEAR:

IN THIS YEAR, WHICH ALT ROCK, POST GRUNGE SINGER/SONGWRITER RELEASED THE ALBUM, "SUPPOSED FORMER INFATUATION JUNKIE"?

IN THIS YEAR, BILLIE PIPER BECOMES THE YOUNGEST BRITISH SOLO ARTIST TO DEBUT AT NO.1 IN THE UK WITH WHICH SINGLE?

IN THIS YEAR, THE MOST PLAYED SONG ON US AIRWAVES WAS BY THE GOO GOO DOLLS. WHAT WAS IT CALLED?

DMX RELEASED HIS DEBUT RAP ALBUM "IT'S DARK AND HELL IS HOT" IN THIS YEAR. WHAT'S DMX'S REAL NAME?

THE MOST SUCCESSFUL SINGLE OF THIS YEAR WAS THE THEME SONG FOR A MASSIVE BLOCKBUSTER MOVIE, SUNG BY CELINE DION, WHAT WAS IT?

NAME THE YEAR:

IN THIS YEAR THE "ROCK AND ROLL HALL OF FAME" INDUCTED IT'S FIRST WOMAN. WHO WAS SHE?

THE US'S 1ST COMMERCIALLY RELEASED CASSETTE SINGLE WAS RELEASED IN THIS YEAR. TITLED "HEAT OF THE NIGHT", WHO SANG IT?

"SWEET CHILDREN" WERE FORMED IN THIS YEAR. BEFORE THEIR 1ST SINGLE RELEASE "1000 HOURS", THEY CHANGED THEIR NAME TO WHAT?

IN THIS YEAR, WHICH LEGENDARY REGGAE ARTIST AND ORIGINAL WAILER WAS TRAGICALLY MURDERED IN A HOME INVASION?

GEORGE MICHAEL WON A GRAMMY FOR "ALBUM OF THE YEAR" IN THIS YEAR. WHAT WAS THE ALBUM CALLED?

NAME THE YEAR:

12

THE MOST SUCCESSFUL WORLDWIDE SINGLE OF THIS YEAR WAS "I CAN HELP". WHO SUNG IT?

CRITICALLY PANNED ON RELEASE, IT'S NOW CONSIDERED A CLASSIC. WHICH MUSICAL COMEDY HORROR FILM WAS RELEASED THIS YEAR?

RICHIE BLACKMORE, FORMERLY OF "DEEP PURPLE" FORMS WHICH BAND IN THIS YEAR?

DAVID BYRNE, CHRIZ FRANTZ, TINA WEYMOUTH AND JERRY HARRISON FORM WHICH US ROCK BAND IN THIS YEAR?

IN THIS YEAR, STEVE HARRIS FORMS WHICH HEAVY METAL BAND?

NAME THE YEAR:

THIS FEMALE SOUL GROUP PERFORMED FOR THE LAST TIME, AT THE FRONTIER HOTEL IN LAS VEGAS. WHO WERE THE GROUP?

ON MARCH 19TH OF THIS YEAR, ANGELA BARNETT MARRIED WHICH SINGER/SONGWRITER?

WIDELY REGARDED AS ONE OF THE WORLDS MOST INFLUENTIAL GUITARISTS, WHO TRAGICALLY DIED IN THIS YEAR?

WHICH BAND "THE MOST INFLUENTIAL OF ALL TIME" OFFICIALLY SPLIT UP IN THIS YEAR AFTER 10 YEARS TOGETHER?

WHICH US MUSIC COUNTDOWN SHOW DEBUTED IN THIS YEAR?

NAME THE YEAR:

SPIZZENERGI TOPPED THE FIRST EVER UK INDIE SINGLES CHART IN THIS YEAR. WHAT WAS THE SONG?

PAUL MCCARTNEY IS RELEASED FROM JAIL AND KICKED OUT OF WHICH COUNTRY IN THIS YEAR?

IN THIS YEAR UK HEAVY METAL BAND IRON MAIDEN RELEASE THEIR DEBUT ALBUM. WHAT WAS IT CALLED?

IN THIS YEAR SINGER IAN CURTIS TRAGICALLY DIED. A YEAR LATER, THE REMAINING BAND MEMBERS CHANGE THEIR NAME TO WHAT?

DARBY CRASH TRAGICALLY DIED IN THIS YEAR. HE WAS THE LEADER OF WHICH L.A. PUNK BAND THAT BRIEFLY INCLUDED BELINDA CARLISLE?

NAME THE YEAR:

IN THIS YEAR TUPAC SHAKUR RELEASED THE FIRST EVER RAP DOUBLE ALBUM. IT ACHIEVED PLATINUM STATUS WITHIN 4 HOURS OF RELEASE. NAME IT.

WHICH UK SINGING GROUP RELEASED THEIR DEBUT SINGLE "WANNABE" IN THIS YEAR THAT HIT NO.1 IN 37 COUNTRIES?

IN THIS YEAR, "PIES DESCALZOS" WAS THE INTERNATIONAL BREAKTHROUGH ALBUM FOR THIS ARTIST, NOW A GLOBAL SUPERSTAR. WHO IS SHE?

MARSHALL BRUCE MATHERS III RELEASED HIS DEBUT STUDIO ALBUM IN THIS YEAR, "INFINITE". HOW'S HE KNOWN PROFESSIONALLY?

WHICH FEMALE US SINGER SADLY DIED IN THIS YEAR IN RELATIVE OBSCURITY, ONLY ACHIEVING HUGE WORLDWIDE SUCCESS POSTHUMOUSLY?

NAME THE YEAR:

LISA LOPES OF R&B GROUP TLC TRAGICALLY DIED IN A CAR ACCIDENT IN THIS YEAR. WHAT WAS HER STAGE NAME?

US REALITY TV SHOW, "AMERICAN IDOL" FIRST AIRED IN THIS YEAR. WHO WAS THE FIRST WINNER?

IN THIS YEAR, ROBBIE WILLIAMS SIGNS THE MOST LUCRATIVE CONTRACT EVER FOR A UK MUSICIAN. HOW MUCH WAS IT FOR?

WHICH GIRL GROUP WERE FORMED ON THE UK REALITY TV SHOW "POPSTARS: THE RIVALS" IN THIS YEAR AND WENT ON TO HUGE SUCCESS?

IN THIS YEAR, THE LEAD SINGER, GUITARIST AND FOUNDER OF THE UK PUNK BAND, "THE CLASH" TRAGICALLY DIED. WHO WAS HE?

IN THIS YEAR, WHICH BAND PLAYED AT THE CAVERN CLUB FOR THE FIRST TIME?

WHICH MUSICAL FEATURING "DO-RE-MI" OPENED AT THE PALACE THEATRE IN THE WEST END IN THIS YEAR AND RAN FOR **2385** PERFORMANCES?

HARRY RODGER WEBB STARRED IN THE MUSICAL MOVIE "THE YOUNG ONES" IN THIS YEAR. WHO IS HE PROFESSIONALLY KNOWN AS?

SLIM JIM PHANTOM WAS BORN IN THIS YEAR. HE'S THE DRUMMER WITH WHICH GROUP?

BORN IN THIS YEAR, SHE CAME SECOND TO DANCE TROUPE "DIVERSITY" IN "BRITAIN'S GOT TALENT". WHO IS SHE?

NAME THE YEAR:

18

"WE BELONG TOGETHER" FROM THE LP "THE EMANCIPATION OF MIMI" SPENDS 14 WEEKS AS US NO.1 IN THIS YEAR. WHO SINGS IT?

WHICH RATM/SOUNDGARDEN SUPERGROUP BECOME THE 1ST US ROCK GROUP TO GIVE A FREE OUTDOOR CONCERT IN CUBA IN THIS YEAR?

WHICH AMERICAN IDOL WINNER'S DEBUT SINGLE BECAME THE FIRST COUNTRY SONG TO DEBUT AT NO.1 ON BILLBOARD HOT 100?

ROCK LEGENDS, GINGER, JACK AND ERIC REFORMED FOR THE FINAL TIME FOR A SERIES OF CONCERTS IN THIS YEAR. NAME THE BAND.

"PON DE REPLAY", RELEASED IN THIS YEAR, IS THE DEBUT SINGLE FOR WHICH BARBADIAN SINGER?

NAME THE YEAR:

19

"RANDOM ACCESS MEMORIES" WON "ALBUM OF THE YEAR" AT THIS YEAR'S GRAMMY'S. WHICH FRENCH ELECTRO DUO RECORDED IT?

THE US ROCK BAND "LIVE" RELEASE THEIR 9TH STUDIO ALBUM IN THIS YEAR. IT'S THE ONLY ALBUM THEY RELEASED WITH WHO AS LEAD SINGER?

TAYLOR SWIFT BECAME THE 1ST FEMALE ARTIST IN BILLBOARD HOT **100** HISTORY TO REPLACE HERSELF AT NO.1. WHAT WERE THE SONGS?

IN THE "AMERICAN MUSIC AWARDS" OF THIS YEAR, WHICH UK/IRISH BOY BAND WON "ARTIST OF THE YEAR"?

CARL BARÂT, PETE DOHERTY, JOHN HASSALL AND GARY POWELL REFORMED WHICH UK INDIE ROCK BAND IN THIS YEAR?

NAME THE YEAR:

20

WHO RECORDED THE ALBUM "SOME FINE OLD CHESTNUTS" IN THIS YEAR?

DORIS DAY REACHED NUMBER ONE IN THE US CHARTS IN THIS YEAR WITH WHICH SONG?

WHO REACHED NUMBER ONE IN THE US CHARTS IN THIS YEAR WITH THE SONG "MR. SANDMAN"?

THE "LOUISIANA HAYRIDE" IN THIS YEAR FEATURED THE FIRST RADIO BROADCAST BY WHICH SINGER?

WHO RECORDED THE ALBUM "SONGS FOR YOUNG LOVERS" IN THIS YEAR?

NAME THE YEAR:

IN THIS YEAR, THE GROUP THAT INCLUDED MEMBERS NEIL YOUNG AND STEPHEN STILLS DISBANDED. WHAT WAS THE GROUPS NAME?

"THE NEW YARDBIRDS" GOT TOGETHER IN THIS YEAR. WHAT DID THEY CHANGE THEIR NAME TO?

AN ANIMATED MUSICAL FEATURE FILM BY THE BEATLES WAS RELEASED THIS YEAR, WHAT WAS ITS NAME?

IN THIS YEAR, A BAND CALLED "EARTH" FORMED. THEY WENT ON TO BE PIONEERS OF HEAVY METAL. WHAT DID THEY CHANGE THEIR NAME TO?

JAMES TODD SMITH WAS BORN IN THIS YEAR. WHAT IS HE BETTER KNOWN AS?

NAME THE YEAR:

WHICH MOVIE BOX OFFICE DISASTER WAS CO-WRITTEN BY U2's BONO AND PREMIERED THIS YEAR AT BERLIN FILM FESTIVAL?

THE HEAVY METAL BAND "DISTURBED" RELEASED THEIR DEBUT ALBUM IN THIS YEAR. WHAT WAS IT CALLED?

ONE OF THE BEST SELLING ROCK ALBUM OF THE 21ST CENTURY IS RELEASED THIS YEAR BY LINKIN PARK. WHAT IS IT CALLED?

"CAN'T TAKE ME HOME" WAS THE DEBUT ALBUM, RELEASED THIS YEAR, OF WHICH SINGER?

BORN IN THIS YEAR, SHE'S THE SISTER OF DESTINY AND NEIL AND DAUGHTER OF BILLY AND LETICIA. WHO IS SHE?

NAME THE YEAR:

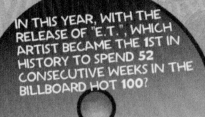

IN THIS YEAR, WITH THE RELEASE OF "E.T.", WHICH ARTIST BECAME THE 1ST IN HISTORY TO SPEND 52 CONSECUTIVE WEEKS IN THE BILLBOARD HOT 100?

WHICH TWO RAP ARTISTS COLLABORATED ON THE ALBUM "WATCH THE THRONE" RELEASED IN THIS YEAR?

30 YEARS AFTER THEIR DEBUT SINGLE "RADIO FREE EUROPE", WHICH BAND AMICABLY BROKE UP IN THIS YEAR?

WHICH RED, WHITE AND BLACK LO-FI GARAGE ROCK DUO SPLIT UP IN THIS YEAR?

JEROME LEIBER OF WHICH LEGENDARY SONGWRITING DUO ADLY DIED IN THIS YEAR?

NAME THE YEAR:

PAUL STANLEY, GENE SIMMONS, PETER CRISS & ACE FREHLEY PLAY THEIR 1ST CONCERT IN THIS YEAR. WHO ARE THEY BETTER KNOWN AS?

IN THIS YEAR THE JOFFREY BALLET'S DEUCE COUPE BALLET OPENS. THE BALLET IS SET ENTIRELY TO MUSIC BY WHICH GROUP?

KING BISCUIT FLOWER HOUR WAS 1ST BROADCAST IN THIS YEAR. A NEW ARTIST ON THE 1ST SHOW IS THE BOSS OF THE E STREET BAND. WHO?

A FAN BITES LOU REED WHERE, DURING A CONCERT IN BUFFALO NEW YORK IN THIS YEAR?

BOB MARLEY AND THE WAILERS RELEASED WHICH ALBUM TO CRITICAL ACCLAIM IN THIS YEAR?

NAME THE YEAR:

WHO, IN THIS YEAR, RECEIVED A "JUKEBOX GLOBAL OSCAR" FOR THE YEAR'S MOST PLAYED ARTIST ON JUKEBOXES?

WHO PLAYED A FOLK SINGER IN "THE MADHOUSE OF CASTLE STREET", A RADIO PLAY FOR THE BBC IN LONDON IN THIS YEAR?

WHICH FAMOUS US FEMALE SINGER WAS TRAGICALLY KILLED IN A PLANE CRASH IN THIS YEAR?

IN THIS YEAR, "COME ON" IS THE DEBUT SINGLE FOR WHICH FAMOUS BRITISH BAND?

MEMBERS OF A SINGLE BAND HAD 6 OUT OF 7 OF THE FIRST UK NUMBER ONE SINGLES OF THIS YEAR. NAME THE BAND.

NAME THE YEAR:

26

WHICH CONTROVERSIAL BAND'S DEBUT SINGLE, "RELAX", WAS RELEASED IN THIS YEAR. BANNED. BECAME 7TH BEST SELLING UK SINGLE OF ALL TIME?

WHICH BAND BROKE EVERY MERCHANDISING RECORD IN CONCERT TOUR HISTORY DURING THEIR "SING BLUE SILVER" TOUR IN THIS YEAR?

THE RECORD FOR THE MOST GRAMMY AWARDS IN A SINGLE YEAR WENT TO MICHAEL JACKSON IN THIS YEAR. HOW MANY DID HE WIN?

WHICH LEGENDARY US SOUL SINGER WAS TRAGICALLY SHOT BY HIS FATHER IN THIS YEAR?

THE CLASSIC TUNE "DIGGI-LOO DIGGI LEY" BY THE "HERRY'S" WON WHICH SINGING COMPETITION IN THIS YEAR?

NAME THE YEAR:

27

IN THIS YEAR, THE ROLLING STONES GIVE A FREE CONCERT TO 1.3 MILLION PEOPLE. WHERE WAS IT?

"SPEED OF SOUND" BY COLDPLAY HAS THE DISTINCTION OF BEING WHAT, ON ITUNES IN THIS YEAR?

SHAFFER CHIMERE SMITH RELEASED HIS FIRST ALBUM IN THIS YEAR - "MY OWN WORDS". WHO IS HE BETTER KNOWN AS?

BON JOVI'S SINGLE "WHO SAYS YOU CAN'T COME HOME" HITS NO.1 IN WHICH US CHART, THE FIRST TIME EVER FOR A ROCK BAND?

IN THE ACADEMY AWARDS OF THIS YEAR, WHICH BAND BECAME THE FIRST HIP HOP BAND TO EVER PERFORM AT THE CEREMONY?

NAME THE YEAR:

IN THIS YEAR, NIRVANA PERFORM THE DEMO OF WHICH SINGLE, DESCRIBED BY MANY CRITICS AS ONE OF THE GREATEST SONGS OF ALL TIME?

FARROKH BULSARA TRAGICALLY DIED THIS YEAR. HE WAS REGARDED AS ONE OF THE GREATEST LEAD SINGERS IN THE HISTORY OF ROCK. BETTER KNOWN AS?

JANET JACKSON BECOMES THE HIGHEST PAID FEMALE RECORDING ARTIST EVER IN THIS YEAR. HOW MUCH DID SHE SIGN THE CONTRACT FOR?

WHILE SISTER JANET BECOMES THE HIGHEST PAID FEMALE RECORDING ARTIST EVER, MICHAEL ALSO SIGNS A CONTRACT IN THIS YEAR. FOR HOW MUCH?

FINALLY, IN THIS YEAR R.E.M. GO FROM CULT STATUS TO MASSIVE INTERNATIONAL ACT WITH THE RELEASE OF THEIR 7TH STUDIO LP, TITLED WHAT?

NAME THE YEAR:

ZACK DE LA ROCHA, TIM COMMERFORD, TOM MORELLO AND BRAD WILK FORM WHICH ROCK/METAL/RAP BAND IN THIS YEAR?

"GISH" WAS THE DEBUT ALBUM IN THIS YEAR FOR WHICH US ALT ROCK BAND WHO WENT ON TO MASSIVE INTERNATIONAL SUCCESS?

WHICH ICONIC US MUSIC FESTIVAL WAS STARTED IN THIS YEAR BY PERRY FARRELL AS A FAREWELL TOUR FOR HIS BAND JANE'S ADDICTION?

WHICH PEARL JAM ALBUM, RELEASED THIS YEAR, INITIALLY SOLD SLOWLY BUT EVENTUALLY WENT ON TO BE CERTIFIED 13XPLATINUM IN THE US?

ON 24TH SEPT. OF THIS YEAR, THE LPS "NEVERMIND", "BLOOD SUGAR SEX MAGIK" AND "BADMOTORFINGER" WERE RELEASED. NAME THE BANDS.

NAME THE YEAR:

IN THIS YEAR STUART SUTCLIFFE JOINED THE BAND "JOHNNY AND THE MOONDOGS". WHAT DID THEY CHANGE THEIR NAME TO?

IN THIS YEAR, ELVIS PRESLEY WAS PROMOTED TO WHICH RANK IN THE US ARMY?

SAMMY DAVIS, JR. MARRIED WHO IN THIS YEAR?

WHICH 14 YEAR OLD FORMED THE GROUP "THE JADES" IN THIS YEAR WITH KEN KOBLUN?

THE SINGER OF "SUMMERTIME BLUES" TRAGICALLY DIES IN THIS YEAR, WHAT WAS HIS NAME?

YOKO ONO MARRIED WHO IN THIS YEAR?

JOHN JOSEPH LYDON WAS BORN IN THIS YEAR, WHAT IS HIS STAGE NAME?

FRANKIE LYMON AND THE TEENAGERS HAD A NUMBER ONE HIT IN THE UK IN THIS YEAR WITH WHICH SONG ABOUT FOOLS?

"SIXTEEN TONS" WAS A NUMBER ONE SINGLE IN THE UK IN THIS YEAR, WHO SANG IT?

THE COASTERS RECORDING CAREER BEGINS THIS YEAR WITH WHICH TUNE?

NAME THE YEAR:

NAMED "THE MOST AWARDED FEMALE ARTIST OF ALL TIME" BY GUINESS WORLD RECORDS, WHICH ARTIST SADLY DIED IN THIS YEAR?

THE BILLBOARD HOT 100 CHRISTMAS NO.1 IN THIS YEAR "LOCKED OUT OF HEAVEN", BY?

THE HALF TIME SHOW OF SUPERBOWL XLVI WAS WATCHED BY 118 MILLION VIEWERS, 6 MILLION MORE THAN THE GAME. NAME THE PERFORMERS.

WHICH ENGLISH SINGER/ACTOR AND MEMBER OF ROCK POP GROUP, THE MONKEES, SADLY DIED IN THIS YEAR?

"GOTYE" IN THIS YEAR AND "THE SINGING NUN" IN 1963 SHARE WHAT DISTINCTION IN THE US SINGLES CHARTS?

NAME THE YEAR:

IN THIS YEAR, WHICH BRITISH MUSIC ICON RELEASED HIS FINAL ALBUM "BLACKSTAR" TWO DAYS BEFORE HE SADLY DIED?

IN THIS YEAR, WHICH RIHANNA ALBUM WAS CERTIFIED PLATINUM IN THE US, 2 DAYS AFTER IT'S RELEASE?

FOR THE 1ST TIME IN 23 YEARS, SAUL HUDSON, MICHAEL MCKAGAN AND WILLIAM BRUCE ROSE JR. PERFORM TOGETHER IN THIS YEAR. NAME THE BAND.

FOR SOME REASON, CELEBRITIES PRETENDING TO SING POPULAR SONGS BECAME A TV SHOW IN THE UK IN THIS YEAR. WHAT WAS IT CALLED?

AFTER THE SAD DEATH OF PETE BURNS, WHICH UK HI-NRG DANCE POP BAND DISBANDED AFTER 36 YEARS?

NAME THE YEAR:

34

IN THIS YEAR, GUITARIST HILLEL SLOVAK TRAGICALLY DIED. HE WAS THE ORIGINAL GUITARIST FOR WHICH BAND?

THE MOST SUCCESSFUL WORLDWIDE SINGLE OF THIS YEAR WAS "A GROOVY KIND OF LOVE" BY WHICH ARTIST?

WHICH CANADIAN ROCK BAND FROM SCARBOROUGH, ONTARIO WAS FORMED IN THIS YEAR BY ED ROBERTSON AND STEVEN PAGE?

"BANG CHAMBER 8" WAS FORMED IN THIS YEAR BY JAMES FRANKS AND MICHAEL BOWE. WHAT DID THEY CHANGE THEIR NAME TO?

IN THIS YEAR, WHICH UK INDIE BAND FORMED THAT A FEW YEARS LATER HEADLINED GLASTONBURY WITH A CROWD OF **300,000** - A RECORD TO THIS DAY?

IN THIS YEAR, WHICH MEMBER OF THE UK ROCK BAND "GENESIS" RELEASED HIS DEBUT SOLO ALBUM, "FACE VALUE"?

WHO HAD A UK NO.1 IN THIS YEAR AFTER APPEARING ON BRITISH TV'S FIRST MUSIC REALITY SHOW?

A SHORT LIVED CRAZE OF MUSIC MEDLEY SINGLES STARTED IN THIS YEAR. WHICH "ACT" WERE THE ORIGINAL PERPETRATORS OF THIS ABOMINATION?

WHICH GENRE OF MUSIC DOMINATED THE UK CHARTS IN THIS YEAR, FROM BANDS SUCH AS ULTRAVOX, OMD, HUMAN LEAGUE, DEPECHE MODE ETC?

THIS COVER VERSION BY SOFT CELL REACHED NO.1 IN 17 COUNTRIES IN THIS YEAR. WHAT WAS IT CALLED? AND WHO ORIGINALLY RECORDED IT?

NAME THE YEAR:

IN THIS YEAR A US PRESIDENT IS CREDITED WITH TWO ALBUMS IN THE TOP **10** SIMULTANEOUSLY. WHICH PRESIDENT?

IN THIS YEAR, AN INDIANA GOVERNOR DECLARED THAT THIS SONG BY THE KINGSMEN WAS PORNOGRAPHIC. (IT WASN'T). WHAT WAS THE SONG?

THE ROLLING STONES RELEASE THEIR DEBUT ALBUM IN THIS YEAR. WHAT WAS IT CALLED IN THE US?

THIS UK GROUP RELEASED FOUR SINGLES IN THEIR DEBUT YEAR. THE FIRST WAS "LONG TALL SALLY". WHO WERE THE BAND?

WHICH MUSICAL, SET IN THE "PALE OF SETTLEMENT OF IMPERIAL RUSSIA," OPENED ON BROADWAY IN THIS YEAR.

NAME THE YEAR:

WHICH FAMOUS LIVERPOOL CLUB OPENED IT'S DOORS FOR THE FIRST TIME IN THIS YEAR?

UK PUNK SINGER SUSAN JANET BALLION WAS BORN IN THIS YEAR. WHO'S SHE KNOWN AS PROFESSIONALLY?

"THAT'LL BE THE DAY" REACHED NUMBER ONE IN THE US BILLBOARD SINGLES CHART IN THIS YEAR. NAME THE BAND.

"QUE SERA, SERA " SUNG BY DORIS DAY IN THIS YEAR WAS FROM WHICH SUSPENSE MOVIE?

WHICH CHESS RECORDS ALBUM WAS THE DEBUT ALBUM FOR CHUCK BERRY IN THIS YEAR?

NAME THE YEAR:

38

NAME THE SINGER BORN IN THIS YEAR WHO BECAME AN INTERNET PHENOMENON WITH THE "RICKROLLING" MEME.

WHICH US MUSICAL VARIETY TV SHOW RAN FROM SEPTEMBER 16TH 1964 TO JANUARY 8TH OF THIS YEAR?

THE DAWN OF THE PSYCHEDELIC ERA IN THE UK WAS HERALDED WITH WHICH YARDBIRDS SINGLE IN THIS YEAR?

IN THIS YEAR, WHICH BAND SET A WORLD RECORD OF HAVING 5 ALBUMS SIMULTANEOUSLY IN THE BILLBOARD POP CHART?

IN THIS YEAR, WHICH US SITCOM'S FIRST EPISODE WAS TITLED "ROYAL FLUSH"?

NAME THE YEAR:

WHICH UK SKA BASED RECORD LABEL, FEATURING "THE SPECIALS", "MADNESS", "THE SELECTER" AND MORE WAS ESTABLISHED IN THIS YEAR?

THE WORLD'S 1ST COMMERCIALLY SUCCESSFUL HIP HOP SONG IS RELEASED BY "THE SUGARHILL GANG" IN THIS YEAR. WHAT'S IT CALLED?

WHICH SINGER, FORMERLY OF "BUFFALO SPRINGFIELD" AND "CROSBY, STILLS, NASH AND YOUNG" BECAME THE 1ST DIGITALLY RECORDED ROCK ARTIST?

WHICH BAND FRONTED BY CHRISSIE HYNDE SIGNED THEIR FIRST RECORDING CONTRACT IN THIS YEAR?

IN THIS YEAR SOMETHING HAPPENED FOR THE FIRST TIME EVER AT THE EUROVISION SONG CONTEST. WHAT WAS IT?

NAME THE YEAR:

40

IN THIS YEAR, BRITNEY SPEARS' MARRIAGE TO A CHILDHOOD FRIEND WAS ANNULLED AFTER 55 HOURS... NAME THE HUSBAND.

WHICH US HARD ROCK SUPERGROUP RELEASED THEIR 1ST ALBUM, "CONTRABAND", IN THIS YEAR?

THE TERM "WARDROBE MALFUNCTION" WAS FIRST USED IN THIS YEAR AFTER SUPER BOWL XXXVIII. WHO SAID IT AND WHO WAS HE REFERRING TO?

WHICH GROUP RELEASED THEIR FINAL LP, TITLED "DESTINY FULFILLED" IN THIS YEAR?

"SOVIET KITSCH" RELEASED THIS YEAR, IS THE MAJOR LABEL DEBUT LP FOR WHICH ARTIST WHO SINGS THE THEME TO "ORANGE IS THE NEW BLACK"?

NAME THE YEAR:

PRISCILLA MARIA VERONICA WHITE, FRIEND OF THE BEATLES, SINGER AND TV PERSONALITY, SADLY DIED THIS YEAR. WHO IS SHE BETTER KNOWN AS?

IN THIS YEAR, WHICH BAND'S SINGLE, "COMING FOR YOU" HIT NO.1 ON THE US MAINSTREAM ROCK CHARTS 18 YEARS AFTER THEIR LAST NO.1?

WHICH ARTISTS DEBUT SINGLE "OCEAN EYES" WAS PUBLISHED ON SOUNDCLOUD IN THIS YEAR, AND COMMERCIALLY RE-RELEASED A YEAR LATER?

WHICH CRITICALLY ACCLAIMED UK ALT ROCK BAND RELEASED THEIR DEBUT LP "MY LOVE IS COOL" IN THIS YEAR?

IN THIS YEAR, MILEY CYRUS RELEASED HER 5TH ALBUM FOR FREE STREAMING ON SOUNDCLOUD. WHAT WAS IT CALLED?

NAME THE YEAR:

IN THIS YEAR, THE ARTIST SELENA BECAME THE FIRST SINGER OF THIS TYPE OF MUSIC TO WIN A GRAMMY AWARD. WHAT IS THE MUSIC STYLE?

THE ALBUM "SMASH" RELEASED THIS YEAR BECAME THE BEST SELLING INDEPENDENT ALBUM OF ALL TIME. WHO RECORDED IT?

WHICH ICONIC GRUNGE BAND LEAD SINGER TRAGICALLY DIED IN THIS YEAR?

IN THIS YEAR, AEORSMITH BECOME THE FIRST EVER MAJOR BAND TO PREMIER A NEW SONG WHERE?

IN THE EUROVISION SONG CONTEST INTERVAL IN THIS YEAR, MICHAEL FLATLEY PERFORMED WHICH WORLD FAMOUS DANCE FOR THE FIRST TIME IN PUBLIC?

NAME THE YEAR:

WHICH MANCHESTER UK INDIE BAND RELEASED THEIR DEBUT LP IN THIS YEAR, REGARDED BY MANY CRITICS AS ONE OF THE GREATEST UK LPS EVER RECORDED?

O'SHEA JACKSON LEFT THE HIP HOP GROUP "N.W.A." IN THIS YEAR. WHO'S HE BETTER KNOWN AS?

ORIGINALLY CALLED "MANIC SUBSIDAL", BY THE TIME THIS PUNK BAND RELEASED THEIR DEBUT US LP IN THIS YEAR THEY WERE KNOWN AS WHAT?

DANA ELAINE OWENS RELEASED HER DEBUT US HIP HOP LP IN THIS YEAR, "ALL HAIL THE QUEEN". WHO'S SHE BETTER KNOW AS?

BORN IN THIS YEAR, NILS SJÖBERG CO-WROTE "THIS IS WHAT YOU CAME FOR" FOR CALVIN HARRIS. WHO IS NILS BETTER KNOWN AS?

NAME THE YEAR:

THE MOST SUCCESSFUL WORLDWIDE SINGLE OF THIS YEAR WAS BY DON MCLEAN, WHAT WAS ITS TITLE?

DAVID BOWIE OPENED WHICH TOUR AT THE TOBY JUG PUB, TOLWORTH, SURREY IN THIS YEAR?

L.A. DJ ROBERT W. MORGAN PLAYS WHICH DONNY OSMOND SONG NON-STOP FOR **90** MINUTES? (POLICE CALLED, NO ARRESTS MADE).

CONSIDERED A "HOLY GRAIL" BY MUSIC COLLECTORS, THIS PSYCH ROCK LP BY "DARK" WAS RELEASED IN THIS YEAR. WHAT WAS THE LP NAME?

BILLY MURCIA TRAGICALLY DIED IN THIS YEAR. HE WAS THE ORIGINAL DRUMMER FOR WHICH INFLUENTIAL GLAM ROCK/PROTO-PUNK BAND?

NAME THE YEAR: 45

BERRY GORDY FOUNDED WHICH WORLD FAMOUS RECORD LABEL IN THIS YEAR?

THE BBC IN THE UK BANNED THE COASTERS SONG "CHARLIE BROWN" IN THIS YEAR BECAUSE OF 1 WORD, WHAT WAS IT?

A TRAGIC PLANE CRASH IN CLEAR LAKE, IOWA THIS YEAR LATER BECAME KNOWN BY DON MCLEAN AS WHAT?

IN THIS YEAR THE GROUP "THE PRIMETTES" WAS FORMED. WHAT DID THEY LATER CHANGE THEIR NAME TO?

THE LEAD SINGER OF "THE CURE" WAS BORN IN THIS YEAR. WHAT IS HIS NAME?

NAME THE YEAR:

46

WHICH IRISH ALT ROCK BAND DISBANDED THIS YEAR AFTER THE TRAGIC DEATH OF THEIR SINGER DOLORES O'RIORDAN THE YEAR BEFORE?

IN THIS YEAR, WHICH MUSICIAN BECAME THE FIRST ARTIST BORN IN THE 21ST CENTURY TO TOP THE BILLBOARD 200 LP CHART?

WHICH BOX-OFFICE MUSICAL MOVIE DISASTER WAS RELEASED THIS YEAR, STARRING JAMES CORDEN AND DAME JUDIE DENCH?

IN THIS YEAR, AFTER 40 YEARS, WHICH INFLUENTIAL UK SKA BAND FINALLY HAD THEIR FIRST UK NO.1 ALBUM, "ENCORE"?

SHE STARRED IN "GREASE" IN 1978 AND IN THIS YEAR IS MADE A DAME COMMANDER OF THE ORDER OF THE BRITISH EMPIRE. WHO IS SHE?

NAME THE YEAR:

IN THIS YEAR BRITISH ARTIST PETULA CLARK REACHES NUMBER ONE IN THE US SINGLES CHART WITH WHICH SONG?

TOSCA, AT THE ROYAL OPERA HOUSE, COVENT GARDEN MARKED THE LAST PERFORMANCE BY WHICH US BORN SOPRANO?

WHICH ICONIC "MOD" GROUP RELEASED THEIR DEBUT SINGLE, "WATCHCHA GONNA DO ABOUT IT" IN THIS YEAR?

ROBBY KRIEGER AND JOHN DENSMORE ARE AMONG THE MEMBERS OF WHICH BAND THAT FORMED THIS YEAR?

WHICH GROUP FORMED THIS YEAR IN PALO ALTO, CALIFORNIA? THEIR FANS WERE KNOWN AS DEADHEADS.

NAME THE YEAR:

48

IN THIS YEAR, CHESTER BENNINGTON BECAME LEAD VOCALIST FOR WHICH US ROCK BAND?

TWO OF ADELE'S SINGLES WERE CERTIFIED PLATINUM IN THE UK IN THIS YEAR. NAME THEM.

IN THIS YEAR, ROBBIE WILLIAMS' ALBUM "SWINGS BOTH WAYS" REACHES NO.1 IN THE UK ALBUMS CHART. WHAT CHART DISTINCTION DOES IT HOLD?

WHICH SCOTTISH SINGER SONGWRITER WON "BRITISH FEMALE SOLO ARTIST" AT THE BRIT AWARDS IN THIS YEAR?

ACADEMY AWARD WINNING MOVIE "HER", RELEASED THIS YEAR, FEATURED A MUSICAL SCORE BY WHICH CANADIAN ROCK BAND?

NAME THE YEAR:

MARCH 19TH OF THIS YEAR, WHO RELEASED HIS DEBUT FOLK ALBUM?

THIS SONG WAS THE FIRST BY A BRITISH GROUP TO EVER REACH NO.1 ON THE BILLBOARD TOP 100 IN THE US. WHAT WAS IT?

THE BEATLES RELEASE THEIR FIRST SINGLE WITH THE CLASSIC BAND LINE UP. WHAT WAS IT (A AND B SIDES).

A DANCE CRAZE IN THIS YEAR WAS FIRST MENTIONED IN "DO YOU LOVE ME" BY "THE CONTOURS". WHAT WAS IT CALLED?

THE MUSICAL FILM "PLAY IT COOL" WAS RELEASED IN THE UK THIS YEAR. IT WAS THIS SINGING STAR'S MOVIE DEBUT. WHO WAS IT?

NAME THE YEAR:

50

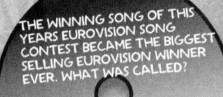

THE WINNING SONG OF THIS YEARS EUROVISION SONG CONTEST BECAME THE BIGGEST SELLING EUROVISION WINNER EVER. WHAT WAS CALLED?

IN THIS YEAR, THE BAND "FEEDBACK" WAS FORMED. WHAT DID THEY LATER CHANGE THEIR NAME TO?

IN THIS YEAR, GEORGE CLINTON HEADS ONE OF THE BIGGEST STAGE SHOWS IN THE HISTORY OF MUSIC. WHAT WAS THE SHOW CALLED?

IN THIS YEAR, THE INFLUENTIAL UK BAND "THE DAMNED" BECAME THE FIRST UK PUNK BAND TO RELEASE A SINGLE. WHAT WAS IT CALLED?

WHICH GANGSTER MUSICAL COMEDY MOVIE FEATURING ALL CHILD ACTORS WAS RELEASED IN THIS YEAR?

NAME THE YEAR:

U2'S 3RD ALBUM "WAR" DEBUTS AT NO.1 IN THE UK IN THIS YEAR. THE ALBUM FEATURED THEIR FIRST INTERNATIONAL HIT SINGLE. WHAT WAS IT?

IN THIS YEAR, WHICH MUSIC MEDIA FORMAT FIRST WENT ON SALE IN THE US?

WHICH MEMBER OF METALLICA IS KICKED OUT OF THE BAND ON THE VERGE OF THEM RECORDING THEIR DEBUT ALBUM IN THIS YEAR?

ELLEN TAAFE ZWILICH BECOMES THE FIRST WOMAN TO WIN WHICH MUSIC AWARD IN THIS YEAR?

IN THIS YEAR, DURING A PERFORMANCE OF "BILLIE JEAN," MICHAEL JACKSON UNVEILS WHICH DANCE MOVE FOR THE FIRST TIME?

NAME THE YEAR:

IN THIS YEAR, WHICH WELSH BAND BECAME THE 1ST WESTERN ROCK BAND TO PLAY IN CUBA (WATCHED BY FIDEL CASTRO)?

THE WORLD'S MOST SUCCESSFUL VIRTUAL BAND RELEASED THEIR DEBUT LP IN THIS YEAR. WHAT ARE THEY CALLED?

IN THIS YEAR, COLIN BLUNSTONE AND ROD ARGENT PLAY TOGETHER FOR THE 1ST TIME IN OVER **30** YEARS. WHICH 60'S BAND WERE THEY IN?

TRAGICALLY, "THE QUIET BEATLE" DIED IN THIS YEAR. WHAT WAS HIS NAME?

WHICH BLUEGRASS BAND'S DEBUT LP, "A HILLBILLY TRIBUTE TO AC/DC" WAS RELEASED IN THIS YEAR?

NAME THE YEAR:

THE BEST SELLING ALBUM GLOBALLY IN THIS YEAR WAS BY AVRIL LAVIGNE. WHAT WAS IT CALLED?

WHICH UK/US BAND, FRONTED BY GORDON SUMNER, REFORMED FOR THE 49TH GRAMMY'S AND A REUNION TOUR IN THIS YEAR?

WHICH VENUE IN NEW YORK DOES ELTON JOHN PLAY AT FOR THE 60TH TIME TO CELEBRATE HIS 60TH BIRTHDAY IN THIS YEAR?

WHICH ARTIST'S SECOND, AND FINAL, ALBUM TITLED "BACK TO BLACK" WAS RELEASED IN THIS YEAR TO WORLDWIDE ACCLAIM AND SUCCESS?

RADIOHEAD RELEASE THE ALBUM "IN RAINBOWS" FOR DIGITAL DOWNLOAD IN THIS YEAR. HOW MUCH DID THE DOWNLOADS COST?

NAME THE YEAR:

54

IN THIS YEAR, SIOBHAN FAHEY REJOIND THE OTHER TWO ORIGINAL MEMBERS OF WHICH INTERNATIONALLY SUCCESSFUL BAND FOR A WORLD TOUR?

THE BEST SELLING ALBUM IN THE UK THIS YEAR WAS BY ED SHEERAN. WHAT WAS IT CALLED?

IN THIS YEAR, HARRY STYLES, FORMERLY OF ONE DIRECTION RELEASED HIS DEBUT SOLO LP, WHAT WAS IT CALLED?

WHICH UK HIP HOP, GRIME, R&B ARTIST RELEASED HIS CRITICALLY ACCLAIMED DEBUT STUDIO ALBUM IN THIS YEAR, "GANG SIGNS & PRAYERS"?

50 YEARS AFTER IT TOPPED THE UK CHARTS, THIS ALBUM WAS RE-RELEASED IN THIS YEAR AND REACHED NO.1 AGAIN. NAME THE ALBUM.

IN THIS YEAR JONI MITCHELL RELEASES HER MOST SUCCESSFUL ALBUM, SUPPORTED BY THE SINGLE "HELP ME". WHAT WAS IT CALLED?

RUSH RELEASED THEIR DEBUT ALBUM IN THIS YEAR. WHAT WAS IT CALLED?

ARGUABLY THE FIRST PUNK BAND, THEY FORMED THIS YEAR IN FOREST HILLS, QUEENS, NEW YORK CITY. NAME THE BAND.

WHICH SWEDISH GROUP WON THE EUROVISION SONG CONTEST IN THIS YEAR?

PORTUGAL'S ENTRY IN THE EUROVISION SONG CONTEST IN THIS YEAR WAS USED ON THE RADIO AS A SECRET SIGNAL FOR WHAT?

NAME THE YEAR:

JOHNNY CASH RECORDED WHICH SONG AT SAN QUENTIN STATE PRISON, FOR THE ALBUM "AT SAN QUENTIN"?

WHO'S DEBUT AND MOST WELL KNOWN ALBUM, RELEASED THIS YEAR, WAS TITLED - "MOTOR-CYCLE"?

IN THIS YEAR "THE WINSTONS" RELEASE "AMEN BROTHER". WHY DID IT BECOME SO SPECIAL?

WHICH ENGLISH ROCK SUPERGROUP, FEATURING STEVE WINWOOD, ERIC CLAPTON, GINGER BAKER AND RIC GRECH FORMED IN THIS YEAR?

IN THIS YEAR ONE OF THE FIRST JAZZ/ROCK FUSION ALBUMS WAS RELEASED BY MILES DAVIS. WHAT WAS IT CALLED?

NAME THE YEAR:

IN THIS YEAR, SOUTH AFRICA BANNED STEVIE WONDER'S MUSIC AFTER HE DEDICATED HIS OSCAR TO WHICH FAMOUS REVOLUTIONARY?

WHITNEY HOUSTON RELEASED HER SELF-TITLED DEBUT ALBUM IN THIS YEAR. HOW MANY US NO.1 SINGLES CAME FROM IT?

WHICH DUO BECAME THE FIRST WESTERN POP GROUP TO PERFORM IN CHINA IN THIS YEAR?

IN THIS YEAR, THE ALBUM "BROTHERS IN ARMS" BY WHICH BAND, SOLD FOR THE FIRST TIME IN HISTORY MORE CD'S THAN VINYL RECORDS?

IN THIS YEAR, WHICH CHARITY MUSIC CONCERTS, THE LARGEST TV BROADCASTS OF ALL TIME AND SEEN BY *1.9* BILLION PEOPLE, TOOK PLACE?

NAME THE YEAR:

20TH JUNE OF THIS YEAR SEES WHAT EVENT TAKE PLACE IN SOUTH WEST ENGLAND DURING THE SUMMER SOLSTICE?

THE BEST SELLING SINGLE OF THE YEAR IN THE UK THIS YEAR WAS SUNG BY GEORGE HARRISON. WHAT WAS THE SONG?

THE LEAD SINGER/SONGWRITER WITH "TAKE THAT" WAS BORN IN THIS YEAR. WHAT'S HIS NAME?

JULY 3RD THIS YEAR SEES THE TRAGIC DEATH OF THE LEAD SINGER OF "THE DOORS". NAME HIM.

IN THIS YEAR, JOHN DEACON JOINS THIS BAND, COMPLETING THE LINE UP. NAME THE BAND.

NAME THE YEAR:

IN THIS YEAR, "JUST DANCE" TOOK **22** WEEKS TO CLIMB TO NO.**1** IN THE BILLBOARD TOP **100**. IT WAS THE DEBUT SINGLE FOR WHICH ARTIST?

A CONCERT NAMED "WE ARE ONE" WAS HELD IN THIS YEAR AS A CELEBRATION OF WHAT?

AT THE US SUPERBOWL XLIII IN THIS YEAR, FAITH HILL, BRUCE SPRINGSTEEN AND WHO, ALL PERFORM AT THE SHOW?

AT THIS YEAR'S GRAMMY AWARDS WHICH ENGLISH SINGER/SONGWRITER WINS THE FIRST OF HER **15** CAREER GRAMMY'S AS OF **2020**?

EMINEM, DR. DRE AND **50** CENT SET A RECORD OF **418,000** DOWNLOAD SALES IN AN OPENING WEEK IN THIS YEAR, FOR WHAT SONG?

NAME THE YEAR:

IN THIS YEAR, VINCE NEAL LEAVES "MÖTLEY CRÜE" AFTER 11 YEARS AS THEIR LEAD SINGER. WHY DID HE LEAVE?

IN THIS YEAR, WHICH MAJOR US ARTIST WAS THE 1ST TO TOUR SOUTH AFRICA AFTER THE START OF THE END OF IT'S DISGUSTING APARTHEID REGIME?

WHICH GUNS N' ROSES SINGLE ENTERED THE RECORD BOOKS AS THE LONGEST SINGLE (NEARLY 9 MINUTES) TO REACH THE US TOP 20 IN THIS YEAR?

ICE-T ANNOUNCES THAT CONTROVERSIAL TRACK "COP KILLER" IS BEING PULLED FROM WHICH BANDS DEBUT LP IN THIS YEAR?

MARK HOPPUS, SCOTT RAYNOR AND TOM DELONGE PUT A US PUNK BAND TOGETHER IN THIS YEAR. WHAT WERE THEY EVENTUALLY CALLED?

NAME THE YEAR:

IN THIS YEAR, WHICH MEGASTAR SINGER RELEASED HER DEBUT SINGLE - "EVERYBODY"?

IN THIS YEAR, WHICH T.S. ELIOT INSPIRED MUSICAL COMPOSED B ANDREW LLOYD WEBBER STARTED AN **18** YEAR RUN ON BROADWAY?

IN THIS YEAR, WHICH LEGENDARY ARTIST RELEASED THE GREATEST SELLING ALBUM OF ALL TIME, AND WHAT WAS IT CALLED?

THE MOST SUCCESSFUL GROUP OF THE **1970**'S, ABBA RELEASE THEIR FINAL ORIGINAL SINGLE IN THIS YEAR. WHAT'S IT CALLED?

THE WORLD'S BEST SELLING SINGLE OF THIS YEAR WAS BY "SURVIVOR". WHAT'S THE SONG AND WHICH MOVIE WAS IT THE THEME TUNE FOR?

NAME THE YEAR:

IN THIS YEAR, WHICH INFLUENTIAL SINGER/RAPPER MADE HISTORY BY BEING THE FIRST FEMALE ARTIST TO WIN 5 GRAMMY'S IN ONE NIGHT?

WHICH CERTIFICATION LEVEL, INTRODUCED THIS YEAR, IS FOR US SALES OF LPS OR SINGLES THAT TOP 10 MILLION UNITS?

IN THIS YEAR, WHICH FAMOUS PEER-TO-PEER FILE SHARING NETWORK WAS LAUNCHED?

"GENIE IN A BOTTLE", RELEASED THIS YEAR, WAS THE DEBUT SINGLE FOR WHICH SINGER WHO BECAME ONE OF THE WORLD'S BEST SELLING ARTISTS?

IN THIS YEAR, WHICH MAJOR US MUSIC FESTIVAL, FOUNDED BY PAUL TOLLETT AND RICK VAN SANTEN, MADE IT'S DEBUT IN CALIFORNIA?

NAME THE YEAR:

THE "BEE GEES" HAD TWO IN THE TOP FIVE OF THE WORLDS BEST SELLING SINGLES IN THIS YEAR. WHAT WERE THEY?

IN THIS YEAR, TED NUGENT AUTOGRAPHS A FAN'S ARM WITH WHAT TYPE OF KNIFE(!)?

ONE OF THE WORLD'S GREATEST, AND MOST PROLIFIC, ARTISTS RELEASED HIS DEBUT LP IN THIS YEAR - "FOR YOU". NAME THE ARTIST.

WHICH INFLUENTIAL POLITICAL HARDCORE PUNK BAND LEAD BY JELLO BIAFRA FORMED IN SAN FRANCISCO IN THIS YEAR?

IN THIS YEAR IRON MAIDEN RECORD A 4 SONG DEMO. WHAT DID THE DEMO EVENTUALLY BECOME KNOWN AS?

NAME THE YEAR:

WHICH BRITISH BAND WITH AN AMERICAN SINGER WON THIS YEAR'S EUROVISION SONG CONTEST WITH "LOVE SHINE A LIGHT"?

IDM BAND APHEX TWIN'S VIDEO FOR WHICH SINGLE IN THIS YEAR WAS BANNED BY UK TV NETWORKS FOR BEING "TOO FRIGHTENING"?

IN THIS YEAR, TINKY WINKY, DIPSY, LAA-LAA AND PO HAD A UK NO.1 SINGLE. WHO WERE THEY KNOWN AS?

THE BEST SELLING ALBUM IN THE UK IN THIS YEAR WAS BY OASIS. WHAT WAS THE TITLE?

IN THIS YEAR, BEN AND JERRY'S INTRODUCE A CHOCCY ICE CREAM, MARSHMALLOW, CARAMEL AND FUDGE CONCOCTION NAMED AFTER WHICH BAND?

NAME THE YEAR:

IN THIS YEAR, THE UK HAD THEIR WORST EVER RESULT IN THE EUROVISION SONG CONTEST WITH ZERO POINTS. WHAT WAS THE SONG CALLED?

WHICH NINE INCH NAILS TRACK DID JOHNNY CASH RELEASE IN THIS YEAR, EARNING HIM A GRAMMY AWARD FOR THE VIDEO?

ROCK BAND EVANESCENCE RELEASED THEIR DEBUT ALBUM (NOT INC. DEMOS) IN THIS YEAR. WHAT WAS IT CALLED?

WHICH ARTIST RELEASED HER DEBUT SOLO ALBUM "DANGEROUSLY IN LOVE" THIS YEAR, WHICH EARNED HER 5 GRAMMY'S IN A SINGLE NIGHT?

SAUL MILTON AND WILL KENNARD FORMED WHICH INFLUENTIAL UK DRUM AND BASS DUO IN THIS YEAR?

NAME THE YEAR:

IN THIS YEAR, THE UK HAD THEIR WORST EVER RESULT IN THE EUROVISION SONG CONTEST WITH ZERO POINTS. WHAT WAS THE SONG CALLED?

WHICH NINE INCH NAILS TRACK DID JOHNNY CASH RELEASE IN THIS YEAR, EARNING HIM A GRAMMY AWARD FOR THE VIDEO?

ROCK BAND EVANESCENCE RELEASED THEIR DEBUT ALBUM (NOT INC. DEMOS) IN THIS YEAR. WHAT WAS IT CALLED?

WHICH ARTIST RELEASED HER DEBUT SOLO ALBUM "DANGEROUSLY IN LOVE" THIS YEAR, WHICH EARNED HER 5 GRAMMY'S IN A SINGLE NIGHT?

SAUL MILTON AND WILL KENNARD FORMED WHICH INFLUENTIAL UK DRUM AND BASS DUO IN THIS YEAR?

NAME THE YEAR:

NAME THE WELSH ROCK BAND WHO'S GUITARIST, RICHEY JAMES EDWARDS, WENT MISSING IN THIS YEAR AND HAS NEVER BEEN FOUND.

IN THIS YEAR, RAPPER TUPAC SHAKUR BECAME THE 1ST MALE SOLO ARTIST TO HAVE A US NO.1 ALBUM WHILE BEING WHERE?

THE MOST SUCCESSFUL FRENCH LANGUAGE ALBUM OF ALL TIME WAS RELEASED THIS YEAR, TITLED "D'EUX". WHO RECORDED IT?

IN THIS YEAR, THE BEATLES RELEASE THEIR FIRST NEW SINGLE IN OVER **20** YEARS, WHAT IS IT CALLED?

WHICH INDIE BAND RELEASED THE LP "I SHOULD COCO" IN THIS YEAR ON PARLOPHONE, THE BEST SELLING DEBUT ON THE LABEL SINCE THE BEATLES?

NAME THE YEAR:

BORN IN THIS YEAR, SINGER SONGWRITER OF "OLIVER'S ARMY".

FIRST DOCUMENTED USE OF THE TERM "ROCK 'N' ROLL" WAS USED TO PROMOTE WHO'S "ROCK 'N' ROLL JUBILEE" IN THIS YEAR?

WHICH ICONIC GUITAR WAS FIRST PRODUCED IN CALIFORNIA IN THIS YEAR?

BILL HALEY AND HIS COMETS RECORD WHICH FAMOUS SONG FOR DECCA IN THIS YEAR?

ELVIS PRESLEY'S FIRST COMMERCIAL SESSION AT SUN STUDIOS WAS IN THIS YEAR. NAME A SONG THAT WAS RECORDED.

NAME THE YEAR:

ONE OF THE MOST SUCCESSFUL, AND CONTROVERSIAL, SINGLES IN MUSIC HISTORY WAS RELEASED THIS YEAR, "BLURRED LINES", BY WHO?

ALBUM OF THE YEAR AT THE GRAMMY'S THIS YEAR WAS BY UK BAND MUMFORD AND SONS. WHAT WAS IT'S TITLE?

WHICH ICONIC MEMBER OF THE VELVET UNDERGROUND, AND SUCCESSFUL SOLO ARTIST, SADLY PASSED AWAY IN THIS YEAR?

CHERYL, NADINE, SARAH, NICOLA AND KIMBERLEY SPLIT UP IN THIS YEAR. WHAT WAS THEIR GROUP CALLED?

SUCCESSFUL IN THE UK AND US IN THE 1960'S, THE TROGGS LEAD SINGER SADLY DIED IN THIS YEAR, WHAT WAS HIS NAME?

NAME THE YEAR:

70

ROBERT FRIPP FORMED THESE PIONEERS OF PROGRESSIVE ROCK IN THIS YEAR. WHAT WAS THE NAME OF THE BAND?

IN THE US, HOW MANY POP SINGLES WERE RELEASED THIS YEAR? (EARN A POINT FOR **1000** EITHER SIDE :)

THE BIGGEST SELLING FEMALE AUSTRALIAN ARTIST OF ALL TIME WAS BORN IN THIS YEAR. WHO IS SHE?

WHICH MEMBER OF THE ROCK AND ROLL GROUP "THE TEENAGERS" SADLY DIED IN THIS YEAR?

THE BIGGEST SELLING SINGLE IN THE WORLD THIS YEAR WAS BY THE BEATLES. WHAT'S ITS TITLE?

NAME THE YEAR:

SWITZERLAND WIN THE FIRST EVER EUROVION SONG CONTEST WITH WHAT ENTRY?

ERIC GRIFFITHS, PETE SHOTTON AND WHO? FORMED THE GROUP "THE QUARRYMEN" IN THIS YEAR.

HOW MANY NUMBER ONE SINGLES DID ELVIS PRESLEY HAVE IN THE US BILLBOARD CHARTS IN THIS YEAR?

GUY MITCHELL HAD THE CHRISTMAS NUMBER 1 SINGLE IN THE US BILLBOARD CHARTS IN THIS YEAR. NAME THE SONG.

THE "JOY DIVISION" LEAD SINGER WAS BORN IN THIS YEAR, WHAT WAS HIS NAME?

NAME THE YEAR:

THE FIRST WINNER OF REALITY MUSIC SHOW "AMERICAN IDOL" WAS BORN IN THIS YEAR. WHO IS SHE?

THIS IS THE YEAR THE FAMOUS AUSTRALIAN ACTRESS AND RAPPER ABBIE CORNISH WAS BORN. WHAT'S HER RAPPER PSEUDONYM?

"EIN BIßCHEN FRIEDEN" BECAME THE 500TH UK NO.1 SINGLE IN THIS YEAR, SUNG BY NICOLE. WHAT WAS ITS ENGLISH TITLE?

"DEXYS MIDNIGHT RUNNERS" HAD THE MOST SUCCESSFUL UK SINGLE OF THIS YEAR. WHAT WAS THE SINGLE CALLED?

KRAFTWERK WERE THE FIRST GERMAN ARTISTS TO HAVE A NUMBER ONE SINGLE IN THE UK WITH WHICH SINGLE?

NAME THE YEAR:

"THE PROCLAIMERS" TWINS WERE BORN IN THIS YEAR. WHAT ARE THEIR NAMES?

"TELSTAR" BY "THE TORNADOES" WON THE "BEST SELLING A SIDE" AT WHICH MUSIC AWARDS THIS YEAR?

IN THIS YEAR, HER FIRST 3 ALBUMS WERE ALL IN THE BILLBOARD CHARTS AND ALL EVENTUALLY REACHED GOLD STATUS. WHO IS SHE?

THE MOST SUCCESSFUL UK HIT SINGLE OF THIS YEAR WAS "I REMEMBER YOU" BY WHO?

HOW MANY NUMBER ONE SINGLES DID ELVIS PRESLEY HAVE IN THE UK CHARTS IN THIS YEAR?

NAME THE YEAR:

THE MOST SUCCESSFUL WORLDWIDE SINGLE OF THIS YEAR WAS BY ABBA AND WAS THE 1ST SINGLE FROM THE "ARRIVAL" LP. NAME THE SONG.

THE ORIGINAL VERSION OF WHICH MUSICAL ROMANTIC DRAMA MOVIE WAS RELEASED THIS YEAR, RECENTLY RE-MADE STARRING LADY GAGA?

REGINALD KENNETH DWIGHT EARNED HIS FIRST UK NO.1 SINGLE IN THIS YEAR, IN A DUET WITH KIKI DEE. WHO'S HE BETTER KNOWN AS?

IN THIS YEAR THE GROUP "MALICE" PLAYED THEIR FIRST GIGS. WHICH INFLUENTIAL UK NEW WAVE/GOTH BAND DID THEY EVOLVE INTO?

THE 1ST ALBUM EVER CERTIFIED PLATINUM BY THE RIAA WAS RELEASED IN THIS YEAR, BY "THE EAGLES". WHAT WAS IT'S TITLE?

NAME THE YEAR:

RELEASED THIS YEAR, ¡ADIOS AMIGOS! WAS THE 14TH AND FINAL STUDIO ALBUM FROM WHICH LEGENDARY US PUNK BAND?

IRISH SIBLINGS, ANDREA, SHARON, CAROLINE AND JIM RELEASE THEIR DEBUT ALBUM "FORGIVEN, NOT FORGOTTEN" IN THIS YEAR. WHAT'S THEIR BAND NAME?

THE WORLD'S BEST SELLING SINGLE IN THIS YEAR WAS "GANGSTA'S PARADISE" BY WHICH RAP ARTIST?

THE SECOND ALBUM BY UK ROCK BAND RADIOHEAD WAS THE WORLDWIDE BEST ALBUM OF THIS YEAR. WHAT WAS IT CALLED?

MORIAH ROSE PEREIRA WAS BORN IN THIS YEAR. FROM BUBBLEGUM POP TO NU-METAL WHO IS THIS YOUTUBER BETTER KNOWN AS?

NAME THE YEAR:

WHICH GERMAN HAPPY HARDCORE LEGENDS FRONTED BY H.P. BAXXTER PLAY THEIR FIRST CONCERT IN THE US IN THIS YEAR?

WHICH US ALT ROCK BAND, FRONTED BY BRENDON URIE, RELEASED THEIR DEBUT ALBUM IN THIS YEAR?

IN THIS YEAR, MADONNA'S NEW ALBUM WAS RELEASED THAT WENT ON TO REACH NO.1 IN 40 COUNTRIES, A WORLD RECORD. NAME THE ALBUM.

WHICH "RHYTHM GAME" FOR PLAYSTATION 2 WAS RELEASED IN THIS YEAR AND HELPED INCREASE THE RECORD SALES OF MANY ARTISTS?

DMX AND THE BEATLES ARE 2 OF 3 BANDS TO HAVE TWO NO.1 ALBUMS IN THE US CHARTS IN THE SAME YEAR. NAME THE THIRD, IN THIS YEAR.

NAME THE YEAR:

ST PETERS' CHURCH GARDEN FETE HELD THE FIRST MEETING OF WHICH TWO POPULAR MUSIC ICONS IN THIS YEAR?

WHICH ORIGINAL MEMBER OF PUNK BAND "THE CLASH" WAS BORN IN THIS YEAR?

THIS SONG BY ELVIS PRESLEY TOPPED THE US BILBOARD TOP 100 CHARTS FOR 8 WEEKS IN THIS YEAR. NAME THE SONG.

THIS YEAR IN SEPTEMBER SAW THE BROADWAY PREMIER OF WHICH MUSICAL INSPIRED BY ROMEO AND JULIET?

PAUL SIMON AND ART GARFUNKEL BEGIN THEIR RECORDING CAREER WITH "HEY , SCHOOLGIRL" IN THIS YEAR, WHAT DID THEY CALL THEMSELVES?

NAME THE YEAR:

IN THIS YEAR, THE SHIP "MI AMIGO" SINKS IN A STORM. IT WAS THE LOCATION OF WHICH LEGENDARY PIRATE RADIO STATION?

WHICH BRAND OF PORTABLE MEDIA PLAYER FIRST WENT ON SALE IN THE US IN THIS YEAR?

WHICH MUSIC FESTIVAL WAS HELD FOR THE FIRST TIME IN THIS YEAR, AT DONNINGTON PARK, UK, HEADLINED BY RAINBOW?

AT **10:50**PM ON DECEMBER 8TH OF THIS YEAR OUTSIDE THE DAKOTA HOTEL NYC, WHICH MUSIC LEGEND WAS TRAGICALLY SHOT?

IN THIS YEAR A MUSIC INSTRUMENT WAS RELEASED THAT BECAME THE INFLUENTIAL CORNERSTONE OF ELECTRO, DANCE AND HIP HOP. WHAT WAS IT?

NAME THE YEAR:

IN THIS YEAR, WHICH OUTKAST ALBUM BECAME THE FIRST RAP ALBUM TO WIN "ALBUM OF THE YEAR", AT THE 46TH GRAMMY AWARDS?

IN THIS YEAR, WHICH UK BAND'S DEBUT ALBUM CHARTED AT NUMBER ONE, BEATING THE BEATLES AS THE YOUNGEST BAND TO ACHIEVE THIS?

IN THIS YEAR, JAMES HILLIER BLOUNT FORMERLY A CAPTAIN IN THE BRITISH ARMY RELEASED HIS DEBUT LP, A WORLDWIDE HIT. WHAT WAS IT CALLED?

JOSH AND ZAC FARRO, JASON BYNAM, JEREMY DAVIS AND HAYLEY WILLIAMS OFFICIALLY FORMED WHICH US BAND IN THIS YEAR?

NO DOUBT'S LEAD SINGER RELEASED HER FIRST SOLO ALBUM IN THIS YEAR. NAME THE SINGER AND ALBUM.

NAME THE YEAR:

BILLBOARD MAGAZINE REPORT THAT BEATLES RECORDS MAKE UP WHAT PERCENTAGE OF THIS YEARS ENTIRE SINGLES MARKET?

ONE OF THE MOST INFLUENTIAL ROCK BANDS OF THE 20TH CENTURY FORMED IN THIS YEAR WITH LEAD SINGER ROGER DALTREY. WHO ARE THEY?

THE WHO RELEASE THEIR FIRST SINGLE, BUT NOT AS THE WHO. WHAT WAS THEIR NAME AND WHAT WAS THE SINGLE?

WHICH GROUP REACHED THE TOP OF THE BILLBOARD HOT 100 FOR THE FIRST TIME WITH "WHERE DID OUR LOVE GO"

IN THIS YEAR, SONNY AND CHER STARTED PERFORMING TOGETHER, USING WHAT NAME?

NAME THE YEAR:

81

ALAN MCGEE OFFERS WHICH "BRITPOP" BAND A CONTRACT AFTER SEEING THEM PLAY AT "KING TUT'S WAH WAH HUT" IN GLASGOW UK, IN THIS YEAR?

CALVIN CORDOZAR BROADUS JR WAS CHARGED WITH, AND LATER CLEARED OF, MURDER IN THIS YEAR. WHO IS HE BETTER KNOWN AS?

WITH OVER 41 MILLION LP'S SOLD, SHE IS ONE OF THE BEST SELLING FEMALE R&B ARTISTS EVER. HER DEBUT LP WAS IN THIS YEAR. WHO IS SHE?

"I'D DO ANYTHING FOR LOVE (BUT I WON'T DO THAT)", WAS THIS YEARS WORLDS BEST SELLING SINGLE. NAME THE ARTIST.

THIS UK FUNK & ACID JAZZ BAND, FRONTED BY JAY KAY RELEASED THEIR DEBUT LP "EMERGENCY ON PLANET EARTH" IN THIS YEAR. NAME THE BAND

NAME THE YEAR:

82

WHAT EVENT HAPPENED AT MAX YASGUR'S DAIRY FARM IN THIS YEAR?

ONE OF THE WORLDS GREATEST ROCK ARTISTS WAS BORN IN THIS YEAR. STARTED HIS CAREER AS DRUMMER FOR "SCREAM".

WHEN STEVE MARRIOT LEFT THIS GROUP, THEY RECRUITED ROD STEWART AND RONNIE WOOD AND CHANGED THEIR NAME TO WHAT?

"I GOT DEM OL' KOZMIC BLUES AGAIN MAMA!" WAS THE DEBUT SOLO ALBUM BY WHICH ARTIST?

WOTTON BRIDGE IS A SMALL VILLAGE IN THE UK, WHAT HAPPENED THERE ON AUGUST 30TH OF THIS YEAR?

NAME THE YEAR:

KENNY ROGERS RELEASES "THE GAMBLER" SINGLE IN THIS YEAR. HOW MANY MOVIES DID HE STAR IN, BASED AROUND THE SONG?

NEW WAVE OF BRITISH HEAVY METAL BAND "DEF LEPPARD" RECRUIT DRUMMER RICK ALLEN IN THIS YEAR. HOW OLD WAS HE?

IN THIS YEAR, WHICH "WINGS" SINGLE BECAME THE BIGGEST SELLING SINGLE IN UK HISTORY UP TO THAT POINT?

IN THIS YEAR, CATHERINE BUSH BECAME THE FIRST WOMAN IN UK CHART HISTORY TO REACH NO.1 WITH A SELF-WRITTEN SONG. WHAT WAS IT?

IN THIS YEAR, "GENERATION X" RELEASED THEIR DEBUT ALBUM. WHO WAS THE LEAD SINGER?

NAME THE YEAR:

WHICH INFLUENTIAL UK ELECTRONIC MUSIC PIONEER WENT SOLO THIS YEAR WITH HIS DEBUT LP "THE PLEASURE PRINCIPLE"?

WHICH SONG BY BLONDIE WAS THE WORLD'S MOST SUCCESSFUL SINGLE IN THIS YEAR?

IN THIS YEAR, HOW MANY GRAMMYS DID THE BEE GEES WIN FOR "SATURDAY NIGHT FEVER"?

IN THIS YEAR B.B. KING BECAME THE 1ST BLUES ARTIST TO TOUR WHICH COUNTRY?

MCA RECORDS PAID $20M FOR WHICH RECORD LABEL IN THIS YEAR THAT IT THEN PROMPTLY DISSOLVED?

NAME THE YEAR:

"SO FAR GONE" WAS A MIXTAPE THAT LAUNCHED WHICH CANADIAN RAP ARTIST INTO MAINSTREAM SUCCESS IN THIS YEAR?

WHICH "BRITAIN'S GOT TALENT" SINGER'S RENDITION OF "I DREAMED A DREAM" BECAME A WORLDWIDE SENSATION IN THIS YEAR?

SINGLE "NUMBER ONE" REACHED NUMBER ONE IN THE UK CHARTS IN THIS YEAR. A COLLABORATION BETWEEN N-DUBZ AND WHO?

POSTHUMOUS SALES OF WHICH MUSIC ICON'S LPS, WHO SADLY PASSED AWAY THIS YEAR, MADE HIM THE BEST SELLING ARTIST OF THE YEAR?

IN THIS YEAR, NOEL GALLAGHER LEFT OASIS. THE REST OF THE BAND CONTINUED UNDER WHAT NAME?

NAME THE YEAR:

IN THIS YEAR, VIRGIN RECORDS RELEASED THEIR FIRST ALBUM. WHAT WAS IT CALLED AND WHO WAS IT BY?

IN THIS YEAR, QUEEN RELEASED THEIR DEBUT ALBUM. WHAT WAS IT CALLED?

IN NEW YORK CITY IN THIS YEAR, THIS DJ ORIGINATES THE HIP HOP GENRE. WHAT WAS HIS NAME?

WHICH AUSTRALIAN BAND WAS FORMED IN THIS YEAR BY MALCOLM AND ANGUS YOUNG?

THE WORLD'S BEST SELLING SINGLE OF THIS YEAR WAS BY "THE ROLLING STONES". WHAT WAS ITS TITLE?

NAME THE YEAR:

"STOP! IN THE NAME OF LOVE" IS THE FOURTH US NUMBER ONE BY WHICH GROUP?

"I HOPE I DIE BEFORE I GET OLD" IS A LINE FROM WHICH ICONIC SINGLE RELEASED IN THE UK THIS YEAR?

ROKY ERICKSON, TOMMY HALL AND STACY SUTHERLAND FORMED WHICH GROUP IN THIS YEAR?

ONE OF THE PIONEERING BANDS OF PSYCHEDELIC ROCK FORMED IN SAN FRANCISCO IN THIS YEAR. WHO WERE THEY?

THE WORLDS MOST SUCCESSFUL SINGLE OF THE YEAR WAS BY THE ROLLING STONES. WHAT WAS IT?

NAME THE YEAR:

IN THIS YEAR, WHICH INFLUENCIAL MANCHESTER UK INDIE RECORD LABEL DECLARED BANKRUPTCY AND WAS BOUGHT BY LONDON RECORDS?

WHICH FILE CODING FORMAT FOR DIGITAL AUDIO WAS DEVELOPED IN THIS YEAR?

THIS YEAR'S WORLDWIDE BESTSELLING SINGLE WAS "I WILL ALWAYS LOVE YOU". WHO SANG IT?

IN THIS YEAR, THE WORLDWIDE BEST SELLING ALBUM WAS "AUTOMATIC FOR THE PEOPLE". WHICH BAND RECORDED IT?

CHARLOTTE EMMA AITCHISON WAS BORN IN THE UK IN THIS YEAR. BY WHAT NAME IS SHE KNOWN PROFESSIONALLY?

NAME THE YEAR:

IN THIS YEAR, ABC PREMIERED A NEW SHOW "IN CONCERT". THE 1ST SHOW FEATURED VINCENT DAMON FURNIER. WHAT'S HIS STAGE NAME?

NAME THE BROADWAY MUSICAL PRODUCTION THAT OPENED IN THIS YEAR AND RAN FOR 3388 PERFORMANCES, THE LONGEST RUN EVER AT THAT TIME.

THIS BAND, FRONTED BY VAN MORRISON, SPLIT UP IN THIS YEAR. WHAT WAS THEIR NAME?

THIS BAND, OFTEN REFERRED TO AS "CCR" SPLIT UP IN THIS YEAR. WHAT WAS THEIR NAME?

CHRISTOPHER GEORGE LATORE WALLACE WAS BORN IN THIS YEAR. BY WHAT NAME WAS HE BETTER KNOWN AS?

NAME THE YEAR:

IN THIS YEAR, "THE JUSTIFIED ANCIENTS OF MU MU" RELEASED THEIR DEBUT UK SINGLE. WHICH ACID HOUSE GROUP DID THEY BECOME?

IN THIS YEAR, "THE LOCO-MOTION" SPENDS 7 WEEKS AT NO.1 IN AUSTRALIA. IT'S THE DEBUT SINGLE FOR WHICH FEMALE SINGING SUPERSTAR?

5 US NO.1 SINGLES, THE MOST IN HISTORY, CAME FROM THIS ALBUM BY MICHAEL JACKSON. RELEASED IN THIS YEAR, WHAT'S THE ALBUM TITLE?

THE TOUR EARNINGS OF MICHAEL JACKSON AND U2 COMBINED, MATCHED THE TOTAL TOUR EARNINGS OF PINK FLOYD IN THIS YEAR. HOW MUCH?

IN THIS YEAR, CBS LAUNCHED A US VERSION OF WHICH POPULAR UK MUSIC SHOW?

NAME THE YEAR:

THIS YEAR MARKED THE RISE OF THE BEATLES. HOW MANY UK NUMBER ONES DID THEY HAVE IN THIS YEAR?

"HOW DO YOU DO IT" WAS THE DEBUT SINGLE, AND REACHED THE UK NUMBER ONE, BY WHICH BAND?

THIS SONG REACHED NO. 1 IN THE UK CHARTS IN THIS YEAR. IT'S BEEN SUNG EVER SINCE, BUT MORE THAN USUAL IN **2020**.

IN THIS YEAR A NEW FORMAT FOR PLAYING MUSIC WAS INTRODUCED BY PHILIPS. WHAT WAS IT?

A BRITISH NEWSPAPER FIRST USES THIS TERM TO DESCRIBE BEATLES HYSTERIA. WHAT WAS THE TERM?

NAME THE YEAR:

THE DOORS RELEASED THEIR DEBUT ALBUM IN THIS YEAR, WHAT WAS IT CALLED?

ON FEBRUARY 16TH OF THIS YEAR, DETROIT, MICHIGAN DECLARES WHICH SINGERS "DAY"?

"PIPER AT THE GATES OF DAWN" IS THE DEBUT ALBUM BY WHICH BAND? ALSO, IT WAS THE ONLY ALBUM MADE UNDER THE LEADERSHIP OF WHO?

WHICH MAGAZINE ROLLED OFF THE PRESSES FOR THE FIRST TIME ON OCTOBER 18TH OF THIS YEAR, AT AROUND 5:30PM?

ANOTHER PLANE CRASH TRAGICALLY TAKES ANOTHER MUSICAL LEGEND IN LAKE MONONA, MADISON, WISCONSIN IN THIS YEAR. WHO WAS HE?

NAME THE YEAR:

93

WHICH BAND RELEASED THEIR DEBUT LP "MORE PARTS PER MILLION" ON THE "SUB POP" LABEL IN THIS YEAR?

"FINAL STRAW" WAS THE 3RD ALBUM, BUT MAJOR LABEL DEBUT IN THIS YEAR, THAT SAW WHICH BAND GAIN MAINSTREAM SUCCESS OUTSIDE OF NORTHERN IRELAND?

THE WORLDWIDE TOP SELLING LP IN THIS YEAR WAS "GET RICH OR DIE TRYING", BY WHICH RAPPER?

WHICH SINGER AND BASSIST FOR THE BEE GEES, TRAGICALLY DIED IN THIS YEAR?

WHICH AMERICAN COUNTRY, ROCK N' ROLL, BLUES, FOLK LEGEND, ONE OF THE BEST SELLING ARTISTS OF ALL TIME, SADLY DIED THIS YEAR?

NAME THE YEAR: 94

WHO BIT THE HEAD OFF A DOVE AT A CBS RECORD LABEL MEETING IN L.A. IN THIS YEAR?

IN THIS YEAR, DIANA ROSS SIGNS THE MOST LUCRATIVE RECORDING CONTRACT IN HISTORY AT THAT TIME. HOW MUCH WAS IT FOR?

WHICH UK ROCK MUSIC MAGAZINE PUBLISHED IT'S FIRST ISSUE IN THIS YEAR WITH ANGUS YOUNG OF AC/DC ON THE COVER?

"VIDEO KILLED THE RADIO STAR" BY "THE BUGGLES" IS THE FIRST MUSIC VIDEO TO BE PLAYED ON WHICH CABLE TV CHANNEL IN THIS YEAR?

WHICH SINGLE BY KIM CARNES WAS THE WORLDWIDE BEST SELLING SINGLE THIS YEAR?

NAME THE YEAR:

SHAWN COREY CARTER RELEASED HIS DEBUT ALBUM THIS YEAR, TITLED "REASONABLE DOUBT". BY WHAT NAME IS HE BETTER KNOWN?

THE BAND "XERO" WERE FORMED IN THIS YEAR, THEY BECAME ONE OF THE BEST SELLING ACTS OF THE 21ST CENTURY AFTER CHANGING THEIR NAME TO WHAT?

"FUZZY LOGIC" WAS THE DEBUT ALBUM, RELEASED THIS YEAR, FOR WHICH WELSH ROCK BAND THAT WAS ONCE FRONTED BY ACTOR RHYS IFANS?

THE BIGGEST WORLDWIDE HIT SINGLE OF THIS YEAR WAS "MACARENA". WHO SANG IT?

THE LEADER OF POST PUNK TRIBAL, PSYCHOBILLY BLUES COUNTRY BAND, THE GUN CLUB TRAGICALLY DIED THIS YEAR. WHAT WAS HIS NAME?

WHICH R&B SOUL LEGEND, THE FORMER LEAD SINGER OF "HAROLD MELVIN & THE BLUE NOTES", SADLY DIED IN THIS YEAR?

IN THIS YEAR, TAYLOR SWIFT BECAME THE YOUNGEST EVER WINNER OF "ALBUM OF THE YEAR" AT THE GRAMMY'S. ALBUM TITLE?

WHICH CANADIAN TEEN POP/R&B SINGER'S DEBUT LP "MY WORLD 2.0" DEBUTED AT NO1 ON THE BILLBOARD 200 IN THIS YEAR?

IN THIS YEAR, THE UK "POP JUSTICE 20 QUID MUSIC PRIZE" WAS AWARDED TO EXAMPLE, THE FIRST MALE WINNER, FOR WHICH TRACK?

IN THIS YEAR, MAGNE FURUHOLMEN, PAUL WAAKTAAR-SAVOY AND THEIR LEAD SINGER SPLIT UP. WHAT WORLD FAMOUS BAND ARE THEY KNOWN AS?

ONE OF THE BEST SELLING SINGER SONGWRITERS OF ALL TIME SADLY DIED IN THIS YEAR AGE 81. A COUNTRY/POP LEGEND. WHO IS HE?

"MY LAST BREATH" BY JAMES NEWMAN WAS SELECTED AS UK'S ENTRY IN THIS YEAR'S EUROVISION SONG CONTEST. WHERE DID HE PLACE?

IN THIS YEAR, IN AN ANNUAL BBC POLL OF MUSIC CRITICS AND INDUSTRY BIGWIGS, UK SINGER CELESTE WAS NAMED WHAT?

THE BIGGEST NEW ARTIST DEBUT THIS YEAR ON THE BILLBOARD 200 LP CHART WAS "KID KROW". WHO'S IT BY?

WHICH DYNAMIC AND FLAMBOUYANT INFLUENTIAL SINGER/PIANIST, OFTEN CALLED "THE ARCHITECT OF ROCK AND ROLL." SADLY DIED IN THIS YEAR?

NAME THE YEAR:

THE MOST SUCCESSFUL SONG IN THE WORLD THIS YEAR WAS SUNG BY BOBBY DARIN, ABOUT A KNIFE, WHAT WAS THE SONG TITLE?

IN THE UK DAVID JACOBS PRESENTED THE FIRST EDITION OF WHICH ICONIC MUSIC SHOW IN THIS YEAR?

IN OCTOBER OF THIS YEAR, WHO'S FAMOUS JAZZ CLUB OPENED IN SOHO, LONDON?

LIONEL BART WROTE WHICH SONG FOR CLIFF RICHARD THAT WAS THE BEST SELLING SONG IN THIS YEAR IN THE UK?

"DREAM LOVER" WAS A NUMBER ONE HIT IN THE UK IN THIS YEAR. WHO WAS THE SINGER?

NAME THE YEAR:

IN THIS YEAR, THE DEBUT SINGLE BY PATTIE SMITH BECAME, ARGUABLY, THE FIRST PUNK ROCK SINGLE. WHAT WAS THE TITLE?

ONE OF THE GREATEST EVER PUNK/NEW WAVE BANDS FORMED IN THIS YEAR. MEMBER. INCLUDE CHRIS STEIN AND CLEM BURKE. NAME?

THE BEST SELLING SINGLE IN THE WORLD THIS YEAR WAS BY JAMAICAN ARTIST CARL DOUGLAS. WHAT WAS IT CALLED?

BORN IN THIS YEAR, MARRIED TO DAVID, MEMBER OF "THE SPICE GIRLS". WHO IS SHE?

IN THIS YEAR, WHICH MEMBER OF "THE MAMAS AND THE PAPAS" TRAGICALLY DIED OF A HEART ATTACK?

NAME THE YEAR:

100

IN THIS YEAR, THE LEGEND THAT IS "THE HOFF" RELEASED HIS DEBUT ALBUM. WHAT WAS IT CALLED AND WHAT'S "THE HOFF'S" FULL NAME?

THIS NORWEGIAN SYNTH-POP BAND'S DEBUT ALBUM "HUNTING HIGH AND LOW" WAS RELEASED IN THIS YEAR. NAME THE BAND.

AFTER MICK JONES WAS KICKED OUT OF THE CLASH, HE FORMED "BIG AUDIO DYNAMITE" WHAT WAS THE TITLE OF THEIR DEBUT LP, RELEASED THIS YEAR?

ALSO IN THIS YEAR "THE CLASH" RELEASED THEIR FINAL STUDIO ALBUM. WHAT WAS IT CALLED?

WHICH UK POP ROCK BAND HAD THE MOST SUCCESSFUL WORLDWIDE SINGLE OF THIS YEAR WITH "SHOUT"?

NAME THE YEAR:

THE MOST SUCCESSFUL SONG WRITER IN THE LATE 20TH CENTURY, THIS ARTIST GAVE HER FIRST LIVE PERFORMANCE, AT CARNEGIE HALL. WHO IS SHE?

IN THIS YEAR CHER EARNS HER FIRST SOLO NUMBER ONE HIT IN THE US. WHAT'S IT CALLED?

IN THIS YEAR "YOUR SONG" IS THE FIRST INTERNATIONAL HIT FOR WHICH ARTIST?

LADONNA ADRIAN GAINES BEGINS HER RECORDING CAREER IN THIS YEAR. WHAT WAS HER STAGE NAME?

GLENN FREY, DON HENLEY, BERNIE LEADON AND RANDY MEISNER FORMED WHICH BAND IN THIS YEAR?

NAME THE YEAR:

102

ANASTASIO, GORDON, FISHMAN AND MCCONNELL RELEASED THEIR DEBUT STUDIO LP IN THIS YEAR. WHAT ARE THEY BETTER KNOWN AS?

INFLUENTIAL SKA PUNK BAND THE MIGHTY MIGHTY BOSSTONES RELEASED THEIR DEBUT US ALBUM IN THIS YEAR. WHAT WAS IT CALLED?

RELEASED THIS YEAR BY ALT METAL/GRUNGE BAND SOUNDGARDEN, THIS WAS THEIR MAJOR LABEL DEBUT LP. WHAT WAS IT CALLED?

THIS UK/US SURREAL COMEDY TROUPE RELEASED AN ALBUM OF MUSIC THIS YEAR TO CELEBRATE THEIR 20TH ANNIVERSARY. NAME THE TROUPE.

THE MOST SUCCESSFUL WORLDWIDE SINGLE OF THIS YEAR WAS BY MADONNA. WHAT'S IT'S TITLE?

NAME THE YEAR:

WHICH SONG, RELEASED THIS YEAR BY THE PRETENDERS FEATURED IN WALT'S FAMOUS "DONUT" SCENE IN BREAKING BAD?

NAME THE SOUTH KOREAN ARTIST AND SONG THAT CREATED A WORLDWIDE DANCING PHENOMENON IN THIS YEAR.

ADAM YAUCH SADLY DIED IN THIS YEAR, CAUSING WHICH ICONIC RAP ROCK BAND TO DISBAND AFTER 34 YEARS?

NEIL YOUNG, STEPHEN STILLS AND RICHIE FURAY GOT TOGETHER AGAIN IN THIS YEAR TO BRIEFLY REFORM WHICH GROUP?

"+" WAS THE DEBUT ALBUM, RELEASED THIS YEAR, FOR WHICH UK SINGER SONGWRITER, WHO LATER APPEARED IN GAME OF THRONES?

FOR THE FIRST TIME IN HISTORY 45RPM DISCS OUTSOLD WHAT IN THIS YEAR?

IN THIS YEAR, THE FIRST USE OF A ROCK 'N' ROLL SONG APPEARED IN A MAJOR MOVIE. WHICH MOVIE?

IN THIS YEAR, WHICH MAJOR RECORD LABEL LAUNCHED A MARKETING PLAN CALLED "OPERATION TNT"?

A LONDONER IS FINED FOR "CREATING AN ABOMINABLE NOISE" PLAYING WHICH SONG BY BILL HALEY AND HIS COMETS IN THIS YEAR?

SUN RECORDS RELEASE "FOLSOM PRISON BLUES" BY WHICH ARTIST?

NAME THE YEAR:

105

"ROLLING STONE" RANKED THEM 28TH IN "100 GREATEST ARTISTS OF ALL TIME". WHICH UK PUNK BAND RELEASED THEIR DEBUT LP IN THIS YEAR?

JOHN SIMON RICHIE REPLACES GLEN MATLOCK ON BASS IN THIS YEAR. WHO IS JOHN BETTER KNOWN AS, AND WHAT IS THE UK BAND?

WHICH LEGENDARY US SINGER WAS TRAGICALLY FOUND DEAD IN HIS TENNESSEE HOME IN THIS YEAR?

WHICH BAND FORMED IN THIS YEAR, CONSISTING OF GORDON SUMNER, ANDREW SOMERS AND STEWART COPELAND?

THEIR LATEST LP "ENCORE" DEBUTED AT NO.1 IN THE UK ALBUM CHARTS IN 2019. WHICH SEMINAL SKA/PUNK BAND FORMED IN THIS YEAR?

NAME THE YEAR:

10¢

NUNO DUARTE GIL MENDES BETTENCOURT, BORN IN THIS YEAR IS LEAD GUITARIST WITH WHICH ROCK GROUP?

FREDERICK ALBERT HEATH TRAGICALLY DIED IN A CAR ACCIDENT IN THIS YEAR. WHO WAS HE BETTER KNOWN AS?

IN THIS YEAR A YOUNG SINGER CALLED DAVID JONES CHANGED HIS NAME TO WHAT?

WHICH PSYCHEDELIC SINGLE BY THE BYRDS WAS BANNED IN SEVERAL US STATES FOR ALLEGEDLY CONDONING DRUG USE.

IN THIS YEAR, WOR-FM IN NYC BECAME THE FIRST FM ROCK STATION. WHO WAS THE MAIN DJ?

NAME THE YEAR:

IN THIS YEAR, "VAN HALEN III" LP WAS RELEASED, THEIR **11TH** STUDIO ALBUM. IT WAS THE ONLY LP THEY EVER RELEASED TO FEATURE WHAT?

IN THIS YEAR, HER DEBUT SINGLE " ...BABY ONE MORE TIME" LAUNCHED HER ON THE PATH TO GLOBAL SUPERSTAR NAME THE SINGER.

IN THIS YEAR, THE CHICKS, FORMERLY THE DIXIE CHICKS, RELEASED THEIR DEBUT LP. WHAT WAS IT CALLED?

SERJ TANKIAN, DARON MALAKIAN, SHAVO ODADJIAN AND JOHN DOLMAYEN RELEASED THEIR DEBUT LP IN THIS YEAR. BAND NAME?

THIS WHITE REGGAE ARTIST FROM THE UK WHO DIED IN THIS YEAR IS IN THE GUINESS BOOK OF RECORDS FOR MOST BANNED SONGS (**11**). WHO WAS HE?

NAME THE YEAR:

IN THIS YEAR, 3 BROTHERS AND A COUSIN FORMED WHICH ALT ROCK BAND IN NASHVILLE, TENNESSEE?

PHARRELL WILLIAMS, CHAD HUGO AND SHAY HALEY FORMED WHICH HIP HOP, R&B, ROCK BAND IN THIS YEAR?

FORMED IN THIS YEAR, THIS FEMALE DUO BECAME THE MOST SUCCESSFUL RUSSIAN MUSIC EXPORT OF ALL TIME. WHAT WERE THEY CALLED?

THEY WROTE THE SINGLE "TORN", A BIG WORLDWIDE HIT FOR NATALIE IMBRUGLIA. THEY SPLIT UP IN THIS YEAR. WHAT'S THE BAND NAME?

"SWINGING SIXTIES" ICON, MARY ISABEL CATHERINE BERNADETTE O'BRIEN TRAGICALLY DIED IN THIS YEAR. WHO WAS SHE BETTER KNOW AS?

IN THIS YEAR, WHICH LEAD SINGER OF INFLUENTIAL UK PIONEERS OF ELECTRO BIG BEAT, "THE PRODIGY" TRAGICALLY DIED?

WHICH US SINGER/ACTRESS, WHO'S 1ST LP "YOU'RE MY THRILL" WAS IN 1949 AND LAST LP "MY HEART" IN 2011, SADLY DIED IN THIS YEAR?

WHICH VIRAL TIKTOK COUNTRY RAP SONG WAS COMMERCIALLY RELEASED AND TOPPED THE BILLBOARD HOT 100 FOR A RECORD 19 WEEKS IN THIS YEAR?

THIS CHRISTMAS, WHICH SONG BY MARIAH CAREY FINALLY HIT NO.1 IN THE BILLBOARD HOT 100, 25 YEARS AFTER IT WAS FIRST RELEASED.

"THE MOST SUCCESSFUL SINGLE IN THE UK CHARTS IN THIS YEAR WAS BY LEWIS CAPALDI. WHAT WAS THE SONG?

NAME THE YEAR:

THE MOST SUCCESSFUL BILLBOARD TOP 100 SINGLE OF THIS YEAR, WITH 10 WEEKS AT NO.1 WAS "HAPPY", BY WHO?

FRANCIS WARREN NICHOLLS JR. SADLY DIED IN THIS YEAR. OFTEN CALLED "THE GODFATHER OF HOUSE MUSIC", HOW IS HE BETTER KNOWN?

IN THIS YEAR, WHICH HIGHLY ACCLAIMED UK FEMALE ARTIST ANNOUNCED HER SECOND TOUR, 35 YEARS AFTER HER FIRST?

IN THIS YEAR, A COPY OF WHICH SONG FROM 1967 BY DARRELL BANKS SOLD FOR £14,543, A RECORD FOR A UK RELEASED SINGLE?

WHICH UK DRUM AND BASS BAND WON "BEST BRITISH SINGLE" AT THIS YEARS BRIT AWARDS WITH "WAITING ALL NIGHT"?

NAME THE YEAR:

ONE OF THE "BIG FOUR" THRASH METAL BANDS, WHICH US BAND DID A FAREWELL TOUR IN THIS YEAR AFTER 37 YEARS TOGETHER?

HER DEBUT STUDIO ALBUM THIS YEAR, "INVASION OF PRIVACY", DEBUTED AT NO.1 ON BILLBOARD 200 AND WON MULTIPLE AWARDS. WHO IS SHE

THE "QUEEN OF SOUL" SADLY DIED IN THIS YEAR. WHAT WAS HER NAME?

THE FIRST KOREAN BAND TO TOP THE BILLBOARD 200, IN THIS YEAR, FOLLOWED BY 3 OTHER NO.1 ALBUMS TO DATE, ARE NAMED?

IN THIS YEAR, WHICH ARTIST BECAME THE MOST AWARDED FEMALE ARTIST IN AMERICAN MUSIC AWARDS HISTORY?

NAME THE YEAR:

AUSTRALIAN RAPPER AMETHYST AMELIA KELLY WAS BORN IN THIS YEAR. WHAT IS HER STAGE NAME?

MARTIN BLUNT, ROB COLLINS, JON BROOKES, JON DAY AND BAZ KETLEY FORMED WHICH UK BAND THAT RELEASED THEIR DEBUT LP IN THIS YEAR?

IN THIS YEAR, WHO WON "BEST BRITISH GROUP" AND "BEST BRITISH ALBUM" WITH "THE RAW AND THE COOKED" AT THE BRIT AWARDS?

IN THIS YEAR, METALLICA WIN THE FIRST EVER GRAMMY IN THE CATEGORY OF "BEST METAL PERFORMANCE" FOR WHICH SONG?

IN THIS YEAR, "LAMBADA" BECOMES THE 1ST NON-SPANISH LANGUAGE TUNE TO TOP THE "BILLBOARD HOT LATIN TRACKS" CHART. WHAT LANGUAGE WAS IT?

"DREAMING OUT LOUD" AN ALBUM RELEASED THIS YEAR, WAS THE DEBUT ALBUM FOR WHICH POP ROCK BAND?

IN THIS YEAR, RIHANNA SPENT 10 WEEKS AT NO.1 IN THE UK CHARTS, AND NO1 IN 19 OTHER COUNTRIES, WITH WHICH SONG

WHICH RAP ARTIST RELEASED WHICH ALBUM IN THIS YEAR, FEATURING INTERNATIONAL HITS, "STRONGER", "GOOD LIFE" AND "HOMECOMING"?

R.E.M., THE RONETTES, PATTI SMITH, VAN HALEN AND WHICH HIP HOP GROUP WERE INDUCTED INTO THE ROCK AND ROLL HALL OF FAME IN THIS YEAR?

WHICH UK INDIE ROCK BAND, FRONTED BY FLORENCE WELCH, FORMED IN THIS YEAR?

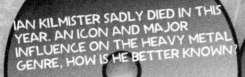

IAN KILMISTER SADLY DIED IN THIS YEAR. AN ICON AND MAJOR INFLUENCE ON THE HEAVY METAL GENRE, HOW IS HE BETTER KNOWN?

A RECORD AT THE TIME, WHICH ADELE MUSIC VIDEO, RELEASED THIS YEAR, GAINED **27.7** MILLION VIEWS ON VEVO IN **24** HOURS?

WHICH UK SINGER SONGWRITER RELEASED HIS DEBUT ALBUM IN THIS YEAR, "CHAOS AND CALM", FEATURING THE SINGLE "HOLD BACK THE RIVER?

WHICH UK ROCK BAND RELEASED THEIR ALBUM "DRONES" IN THIS YEAR, TOPPING **21** INTERNATIONAL CHARTS INC. US AND UK?

IN THIS YEAR, WHICH UK SINGER SONGWRITER WON BEST NEW ARTIST, RECORD, SONG OF THE YEAR AND VOCAL ALBUM AT THE GRAMMY'S?

IN THIS YEAR, WHO JOINED "THE BLACK EYED PEAS" FOR THE RECORDING OF "ELEPHUNK", THEIR THIRD ALBUM?

GEETHALI JONES SHANKAR RELEASED HER DEBUT LP IN THIS YEAR, "COME AWAY WITH ME". HOW IS SHE BETTER KNOWN?

IN THIS YEAR, WHICH "NU-DISCO" US BAND, WHO WERE ALWAYS MORE POPULAR OUTSIDE OF THE US, RELEASED THEIR DEBUT SINGLE?

WHICH CANADIAN POP PUNK SINGER/SONGWRITER RELEASED HER DEBUT LP "LET GO" IN THIS YEAR?

STEVE COOGAN STARRED IN THIS MOVIE, RELEASED THIS YEAR, ABOUT THE MANCHESTER (UK) MUSIC SCENE. WHAT IS IT CALLED?

NAME THE YEAR:

WHICH BAND IN THIS YEAR SIGNED TO EPIC RECORDS, BECOMING THE 1ST BLACK METAL BAND ON A MAJOR RECORD LABEL?

IN THIS YEAR, THE MOST SUCCESSFUL ROCK BAND TO EVER COME OUT OF NEVADA WERE FORMED. WHO ARE THEY?

WIDELY REGARDED BY MANY AS THE "GREATEST DJ OF ALL TIME", WHICH ITALIAN DJ RELEASED HIS DEBUT SOLO ALBUM IN THIS YEAR?

HEAVY METAL BAND, MÖTLEY CRÜE, PUBLISH THEIR AUTOBIOGRAPHY IN THIS YEAR. WHAT'S IT CALLED?

CALLED BY MANY, "PRINCESS OF R&B" AND "QUEEN OF URBAN POP" WHICH SINGER TRAGICALLY DIED IN A PLANE CRASH THIS YEAR?

A CD COPY OF WHICH STING ALBUM BECAME THE 1ST ITEM SECURELY PURCHASED VIA THE INTERNET?

IN THIS YEAR, OASIS RELEASE THEIR DEBUT ALBUM TO GREA SUCCESS. WHAT IS IT'S NAME?

IN THIS YEAR "NU-METAL" IS LAUNCHED INTO THE MAINSTREAM WITH THE RELEASE OF WHICH LP BY THE BAND KORN?

IN THIS YEAR, BLAZE BAYLEY BECAME THE LEAD SINGER OF WHICH LEADING UK HEAVY METAL BAND?

IN THIS YEAR, AFTER THE DEMISE OF NIRVANA, DRUMMER DAVE GROHL FORMED WHICH BAND?

NAME THE YEAR:

118

DAVID BOWIE RELEASED HIS MOST COMMERCIALLY SUCCESSFUL ALBUM IN THIS YEAR, HIS 15TH ALBUM. WHAT WAS IT CALLED?

IN THIS YEAR, WHICH LEAD GUITARIST OF LEGENDARY PUNK BAND, "THE CLASH" WAS KICKED OUT OF THE BAND?

IN THIS YEAR, WHICH LEAD VOCALIST PERFORMED HIS FINAL SHOW IN NUREMBERG, GERMANY WITH THE HARD ROCK BAND THIN LIZZY?

IN THIS YEAR, THE FIRST HEAVY METAL ALBUM TO HIT NO.1 IN THE US CHARTS WAS CALLED "METAL HEALTH". WHICH GROUP WAS IT BY?

THE MOST SUCCESSFUL WORLDWIDE SINGLE OF THIS YEAR WAS "KARMA CHAMELEON". NAME THE GROUP?

IN THIS YEAR THE BEATLES PLAYED THEIR 1ST EVER TOUR, SUPPORTING JOHNNY GENTLE. WHERE DID THE TOUR TAKE PLACE?

IN THIS YEAR, THE LAST OF WHAT TYPES OF RECORDS WERE RELEASED IN THE UK AND USA?

THE BIGGEST HIT SINGLE IN THE WORLD THIS YEAR WAS BY ELVIS PRESLEY. WHAT WAS THE SONG?

AUSTRALIAN SINGER MICHAEL HUTCHENCE WAS BORN IN THIS YEAR, WHICH BAND DID HE FRONT?

BONO, FROM U2 WAS BORN IN THIS YEAR. WHAT'S HIS FULL REAL NAME?

NAME THE YEAR:

THIS BROADWAY MUSICAL, OPENED IN THIS YEAR, HAS THE LONGEST RUN IN BROADWAY HISTORY. WHAT'S IT'S NAME?

WHICH FRENCH CANADIAN SINGER, REPRESENTING SWITZERLAND WON THE EUROVISION SONG CONTEST THIS YEAR WITH "NE PARTEZ PAS SANS MOI"?

WHICH INFLUENTIAL INDUSTRIAL ROCK BAND DID TRENT REZNOR FORM IN THIS YEAR?

"LOVE BUZZ", RELEASED THIS YEAR, WAS THE DEBUT SINGLE FOR WHICH INFLUENTIAL ALT ROCK GRUNGE BAND LEGENDS?

THE FIRST HIP HOP GROUP TO BE INDUCTED INTO THE "ROCK AND ROLL HALL OF FAME" SPLIT UP IN THIS YEAR, WHO WERE THEY?

NAME THE YEAR:

ONE OF THE GREATEST MUSICIANS OF ALL TIME, WHICH PROLIFIC US SINGER SONGWRITER MULTI-INSTRUMENTALIST SADLY DIED THIS YEAR?

SIA IN THIS YEAR AND MADONNA IN **2005** SHARE WHAT DISTINCTION WITH THEIR NO.**1** SINGLES?

Q-TIP, PHIFE DAWG, ALI SHAHEED MUHAMMED AND JAROBI WHITE RELEASE THEIR FINAL ALBUM IN THIS YEAR. WHO ARE THEY?

FOR THE **1ST** TIME IN HISTORY, THE UK SINGLES CHART HAD THE TOP **3** POSITIONS OCCUPIED BY THE SAME ARTIST, ON 14TH JAN. OF THIS YEAR. WHO IS HE?

THE MOST SUCCESSFUL SINGLE IN THIS YEAR IN THE UK WAS "ONE DANCE", BY WHO?

13 YEARS AFTER HIS DISAPPEARANCE, WHICH MANIC STREET PREACHER IS DECLARED "DEAD IN ABSENTIA" IN THIS YEAR?

IN THIS YEAR, BLUR REUNITE FOR A CONCERT IN HYDE PARK, LONDON. HOW LONG DID IT TAKE FOR THE CONCERT TICKETS TO SELL OUT?

WHICH FEMALE SINGER HAD A NO.1 SINGLE IN THIS YEAR, MAKING IT FIVE NO.1 SINGLES FOR HER IN THIS DECADE, TIEING WITH RIHANNA?

THIS DUO SPLIT UP IN THIS YEAR, BUT HAVE HAD MANY REUNIONS. WITH A STYLE SELF-DESCRIBED AS "BRECHTIAN PUNK CABARET", WHO ARE THEY?

THE FIRST AND LAST UK NO.1'S OF THIS YEAR WERE BY LEON JACKSON AND ALEXANDRA BURKE RESPECTIVELY. WHAT DID THEY HAVE IN COMMON?

NAME THE YEAR:

IN THIS YEAR, WHICH HEAVY METAL BAND, FROM WEST BROMWICH UK, WERE BANNED FOR LIFE FROM MADISON SQUARE GARDEN?

THE LATINO BOY BAND MENUDO'S LAST ORIGINAL MEMBER LEFT IN THIS YEAR TO BE REPLACED BY ENRIQUE MARTIN MORALES. WHO'S HE BETTER KNOWN AS?

IN THIS YEAR THE RED HOT CHILI PEPPERS RELEASE THEIR DEBUT ALBUM. WHAT'S IT CALLED?

THE FIRST COMMERCIAL CD EVER MADE IN THE US WAS AN ALBUM BY BRUCE SPRINGSTEEN IN THIS YEAR. WHAT WAS IT CALLED?

THE FASTEST SELLING UK SINGLE OF ALL TIME WAS RELEASED BY "BAND AID" IN THIS YEAR. WHAT WAS THE TITLE?

NAME THE YEAR:

124

WHAT IS THE NAME OF SIMON AND GARFUNKELS LAST ALBUM TOGETHER, RELEASED THIS YEAR AND WINNING A RECORD 6 GRAMMYS?

MANY MUSIC CRITICS CONSIDER THIS ALBUM BY "THE WHO" TO BE THE BEST LIVE ROCK RECORDING OF ALL TIME. WHAT'S IT CALLED?

IN THIS YEAR, RAY DAVIES OF THE KINKS MADE A 6000 MILE ROUND TRIP TO RE-RECORD ONE WORD OF A SONG. WHAT WAS THE SONG?

IN THIS YEAR, THE LARGEST MUSIC FESTIVAL OF ALL TIME WAS HELD AT EAST AFTON FARM IN THE UK. WHAT WAS IT CALLED?

ERIC CLAPTON, BOBBY WHITLOCK, CARL RADLE AND JIM GORDON RELEASED THEIR ONLY ALBUM IN THIS YEAR. WHAT WAS THEIR BAND NAME?

NAME THE YEAR:

UK SINGING GROUP, SUGABABES RELEASE THEIR DEBUT SINGLE IN THIS YEAR. THEY WENT ON TO EARN 6 NO.1 SINGLES. WHAT WAS THE SINGLE CALLED?

THIS UK BAND, FORMERLY CALLED "PECTORALZ", THEN "STARFISH", RELEASED THEIR DEBUT LP IN THIS YEAR, "PARACHUTES". WHO ARE THE

THE MOST SUCCESSFUL WORLDWIDE SINGLE OF THIS YEAR WAS CALLED "MUSIC", WHICH FEMALE SINGER RELEASED IT?

THE BEST SELLING ALBUM IN THE US IN THIS YEAR WITH ALMOST 10 MILLION SALES WAS "NO STRINGS ATTACHED", BY WHICH BOY BAND?

FORMERLY THE LEAD SINGER OF KILBURN AND THE HIGH ROADS, THIS UK POST PUNK ARTIST TRAGICALLY DIED IN THIS YEAR. WHO WAS HE?

NAME THE YEAR:

DUANE EDDY RELEASES HIS DEBUT ALBUM IN THIS YEAR. NAME THE ALBUM.

"GREAT BALLS OF FIRE" WAS THE FIRST UK NUMBER ONE OF THIS YEAR. WHO SANG IT?

IN THIS YEAR, BILLBOARD MAGAZINE LAUNCHED IT'S HOT 100 SINGLES CHART. WHO HAD THE FIRST NUMBER ONE?

"ON THE STREET WHERE YOU LIVE" WAS A UK NUMBER ONE IN THIS YEAR, WHO SANG IT?

OFTEN REFERRED TO AS "THE MODFATHER" WHO IS THE BRITISH MUSIC ICON BORN IN THIS YEAR?

NAME THE YEAR:

THEY BECAME THE FIRST GROUP TO WIN THE UK X FACTOR IN THIS YEAR. WHAT IS THE BAND NAME?

THIS YEARS BRIT AWARDS, BENJAMIN PAUL BALANCE-DREW WON "BRITISH MALE SOL ARTIST". BY WHAT NAME IS HE BETTER KNOWN?

RECORD OF THE YEAR, VOTED FOR BY THE UK PUBLIC, WAS BY LADY GAGA. WHAT WAS THE SONG?

IN THIS YEAR, THE UK NO.1 ALBUM AT CHRISTMAS WAS "CHRISTMAS" BY WHICH CANADIAN CROONER?

IN THE UK IN THIS YEAR, THE BEST SELLING ALBUM AND SINGLE OF THE YEAR WERE BY ADELE. NAME THE ALBUM AND SINGLE.

NAME THE YEAR:

WHICH INFLUENTIAL UK BAND, FRONTED BY STEVEN MORRISSEY, PLAYED THEIR LAST GIG AT THE BRIXTON ACADEMY IN LONDON IN THIS YEAR?

NEIL TENNANT AND CHRIS LOWE RELEASED THEIR DEBUT ALBUM "PLEASE" IN THIS YEAR. WHAT ARE THEY BETTER KNOWN AS?

IN THIS YEAR BRUCE PAVITT AND JONATHAN PONEMAN FOUNDED WHICH ICONIC RECORD LABEL IN SEATTLE, WASHINGTON?

RELEASED THIS YEAR, "HOT, COOL, & VICIOUS" WAS THE 1ST ALBUM BY A FEMALE RAP GROUP TO REACH PLATINUM STATUS IN THE US. WHO ARE THE GROUP?

IN THIS YEAR, "LIVE ?! *@ LIKE A SUICIDE" WAS THE 1ST MUSIC RELEASED BY WHICH LEGENDARY ROCK BAND?

NAME THE YEAR:

129

IN THIS YEAR, THE MOST SUCCESSFUL R&B SONG IN HISTORY SPENT 15 WEEKS AT NO.1 IN THE US BILLBOARD R&B CHART. WHO SANG IT?

A WORLD RECORD IS BROKEN IN THIS YEAR WHEN 1,951 GUITARISTS SIMULTANEOUSL PLAY WHICH JIMI HENDRIX SONG?

IN THIS YEAR'S EUROVISION SONG CONTEST, THE FIRST EVER HARD ROCK ACT IS THE WINNER. NAME THE BAND.

WHICH 16 YEAR OLD SINGER RELEASED HER FIRST SINGLE "TIM MCGRAW" IN THIS YEAR?

THIS YEAR SAW THE LAST EVER WEEKLY EDITION OF WHICH ICONIC UK MUSIC SHOW AFTER 42 YEARS?

NAME THE YEAR:

THE MOST SUCCESSFUL UK SINGLE OF THIS YEAR WAS A ROCK SONG LASTING FOR 6 MINUTES. WHAT WAS IT AND WHO SUNG IT?

WILLIAM ADAMS WAS BORN IN THIS YEAR. WHAT'S HE BETTER KNOWN AS?

IN THIS YEAR, A FILM STARRING THE MEMBERS OF "SLADE" PREMIERES AT THE METROPOLE THEATRE IN LONDON. WHAT WAS IT CALLED?

"THE BEE GEES" BEGIN THEIR MID 70'S INTERNATIONAL COMEBACK IN THIS YEAR WITH WHICH DISCO CLASSIC?

WHICH BAND THAT INITIATED THE UK PUNK MOVEMENT PLAYED THEIR FIRST CONCERT AT ST. MARTIN'S SCHOOL OF ART IN LONDON IN THIS YEAR?

NAME THE YEAR:

"SUPA DUPA FLY" RELEASED IN THE US THIS YEAR, IS THE DEBUT SOLO ALBUM FOR WHICH FEMALE RAPPER/SINGER?

ISAAC, TAYLOR AND ZAC'S DEBUT SINGLE REACHED NO.1 IN 27 COUNTRIES IN THIS YEAR. WHAT WAS THE SONG AND WHO ARE THEY KNOWN AS?

"MO MONEY MO PROBLEMS" REACHES NO.1 IN THE US IN THIS YEAR, MAKING NOTORIOUS B.I.G. THE FIRST ARTIST TO ACHIEVE WHAT?

IN THIS YEAR, UK ROCK BAND THE VERVE RELEASE A SINGLE AND MOST OF ITS ROYALTIES END UP GOING TO THE ROLLING STONES. NAME THE SINGLE.

IN THIS YEAR, CANADIAN SINGER SHANIA TWAIN RELEASED WHICH ALBUM THAT BECAME THE BEST SELLING LP IN COUNTRY MUSIC HISTORY?

NAME THE YEAR:

THE BEST SELLING SINGLE OF THIS YEAR IN THE UK WAS SUNG BY ELVIS PRESLEY. WHAT WAS THE SONG?

IN THIS YEAR, TWO SINGLES REACHED NUMBER ONE IN THE UK WITH THE WORD "MOON" IN THE TITLE. NAME THEM.

IN THE UK THIS YEAR, JOHN LEYTON REACHED NUMBER ONE TWICE WITH THE SAME SONG. NAME THE SONG.

THIS YEAR, BROOK BENTON REACHED NUMBER ONE IN THE NEW BILLBOARD EASY LISTENING CHART. WHAT WAS THE SONG?

THIS YEAR "CANDIX RECORDS" RELEASED THE DEBUT 45: "SURFIN'" BY WHICH GROUP?

NAME THE YEAR:

IN THIS YEAR, WHICH RAPPER BECAME THE FIRST UNSIGNED ARTIST TO EVER WIN A GRAMMY AWARD?

WHICH SOUNDGARDEN AND AUDIOSLAVE FRONTMAN TRAGICALLY DIED IN THIS YEAR?

WHICH COUNTRY LEGEND RELEASED HIS FINAL ALBUM IN THIS YEAR, "ADIÓS"?

ONE OF THE GREATEST ROCK VOCALISTS, SINGER WITH LINKIN PARK AND STONE TEMPLE PILOTS, TRAGICALLY DIED THIS YEAR. WHAT'S HIS NAME?

WHICH MASSIVELY INFLUENTIAL ROCK AND ROLL PIONEER, NICKNAMED "FATHER OF ROCK AND ROLL" SADLY DIED IN THIS YEAR AGED 90?

NAME THE YEAR:

13

ANSWERS

Page 1 - 2018

Damn
Kawaii Metal band, Babymetal
Maddie Poppe
God's Plan
Beerbongs & Bentleys

Page 2 - 1967

Sandie Shaw - Puppet on a String
Randy Scouse Git
Monterey Pop Festival (Mount Tamalpais Festival preceded it by a week but was relatively small scale)
Tangerine Dream
Toots and The Maytals

Page 3 - 1986

Madonna
Q
NKOTB - New Kids on the Block
Rock Me Amadeus
Lady Gaga

Page 4 - 1993

A swarm of grasshoppers invaded the stage
Suede (AKA The London Suede in the US)
The Verve. (At the time just called Verve)
River Phoenix
Enter the Wu-Tang (36 Chambers)

Page 5 - 1958

Phil Spector
Magic Moments
Rock 'n' Roll Music
Conway Twitty
Jools Holland

Page 6 - 1977

The B52's
The Stranglers
Marc Bolan
Adam and the Ants
Stiff Little Fingers

Page 7 - 2008

Leona Lewis
Lil' Wayne
Sticky and Sweet Tour
Donna Summer

Coldplay

Page 8 - 1955

Bill Haly and his Comets
Colonel Tom Parker
Simon and Garfunkel
Maybellene
Fats Domino

Page 9 - 2020

100 (with, You'll Never Walk Alone
Chromatica
Dua Lipa
Her brother FINNEAS - they won 5 each
Genesis P-Orridge (born Neil Andrew Megson)

Page 10 - 2010

Elvis Presley
Hope for Haiti Now
Supergrass
Stevie Wonder
Telephone

Page 11 - 1998

Alanis Morissette
Because we want to (She was 15)
Iris
Earl Simmons
My Heart will go on

Page 12 - 1987

Aretha Franklin
Bryan Adams
Green Day
Peter Tosh
Faith

Page 13 - 1975

Billy Swan
The Rocky Horror Picture Show
Rainbow
Talking Heads
Iron Maiden

Page 14 - 1970

Diana Ross and the Supremes
David Bowie
Jimi Hendrix
The Beatles

American Top 40

Page 15 - 1980

Where's Captain Kirk
Japan
Iron Maiden
New Order
The Germs

Page 16 - 1996

All Eyez on Me
The Spice Girls
Shakira
Eminem
Eva Cassidy

Page 17 - 2002

Left Eye
Kelly Clarkson
£80 million for a 6 album deal
Girls Aloud
Joe Strummer

Page 18 - 1961

The Beatles
The Sound of Music
Cliff Richard
The Stray Cats
Susan Boyle

Page 19 - 2005

Mariah Carey
Audioslave
Carrie Underwood (Inside Your Heaven)
Cream
Rihanna

Page 20 - 2014

Daft Punk
Chris Shinn (Main vocalist - Ed
Kowalczyk)
Shake it Off was replaced by Blank
Space
One Direction (They won it the following
year too)
The Libertines

Page 21 - 1954

Bing Crosby
Secret Love
The Chordettes

Elvis Presley
Frank Sinatra

Page 22 - 1968

Buffalo Springfield
Led Zeppelin
Yellow Submarine
Black Sabbath
LL Cool J

Page 23 - 2000

The Million Dollar Hotel
The Sickness
Hybrid Theory
Pink
Noah Cyrus

Page 24 - 2011

Katy Perry
Jay-Z and Kanye West
R.E.M.
The White Stripes
Leiber and Stoller - writers of over
70 US chart hits

Page 25 - 1973

Kiss
The Beach Boys
Bruce Springsteen
The bottom
Catch a Fire

Page 26 - 1963

Dalida
Bob Dylan
Patsy Cline
The Rolling Stones
Cliff Richard and the Shadows.
(They had 3 No.1's, the Shadows
had 2 and Jet Harris and Tony
Meehan of the Shadows had 1)

Page 27 - 1984

Frankie Goes to Hollywood
Duran Duran
8 (out of 12 nominations)
Marvin Gaye
Eurovision Song Contest

Page 28 - 2006

Rio de Janeiro, Brazil

The One Billionth download
Ne-Yo
It hit No.1 in the US Hot Country Charts
Three 6 Mafia

Page 29 - 1991

Smells Like Teen Spirit
Freddie Mercury
US $30 million
US $1 Billion
Out of Time

Page 30 - 1991

Rage Against the Machine
The Smashing Pumpkins
Lollapalooza
Ten (Their debut album)
Nirvana, Red Hot Chili Peppers,
Soundgarden

Page 31 - 1960

The Beatles
Sergeant
May Britt
Neil Young
Eddie Cochran

Page 32 - 1956

Anthony Cox
Johnny Rotten
Why do Fools fall in Love
Tennessee Ernie Ford
Turtle Down

Page 33 - 2012

Whitney Houston
Bruno Mars
Cee Lo Green, M.I.A. Madonna, LMFAO,
Nicki Minaj
Davy Jones
The only Belgian born artists to reach
No.1 in Billboard Hot 100

Page 34 - 2016

David Bowie
Anti;
Guns N' Roses (Slash, Duff McKagen
and Axl Rose respectively)
Lip Sync Battle: UK
Dead or Alive

Page 35 - 1988

Red Hot Chili Peppers
Phil Collins
Barenaked Ladies
Bloodhound Gang
The Levellers

Page 36 - 1981

Phil Collins
Sheen Easton - Morning Train (9
5)
Stars on 45
Synthpop
Tainted Love - Gloria Jones (1965

Page 37 - 1964

John F. Kennedy
Louie Louie
The Rolling Stones - England's
Newest Hit Makers
The Kinks
Fiddler on the Roof

Page 38 - 1957

Cavern Club
Siouxsie Sioux
The Crickets
The Man who knew Too Much
After School Session

Page 39 - 1966

Rick Astley
Shindig!
Shapes of things / Mister, You're
Better Man than I
Herb Alpert & The Tijuana Brass
The Monkees

Page 40 - 1979

2 Tone Records
Rapper's Delight
Stephen Stills
The Pretenders
It was held outside Europe (Israel

Page 41 - 2004

Jason Allen Alexander
Velvet Revolver
Justin Timberlake said it regardin
Janet Jackson
Destiny's Child
Regina Spektor

Page 42 - 2015

Cilla Black
The Offspring (previous No.1 in 1997 was "Gone Away")
Billie Eilish
Wolf Alice
Miley Cyrus & Her Dead Petz

Page 43 - 1994

Tejano Music (A fusion of Mexican, US and European styles)
The Offspring
Kurt Cobain
The Internet
Riverdance

Page 44 - 1989

The Stone Roses by The Stone Roses
Ice Cube
The Offspring
Queen Latifah
Taylor Swift

Page 45 - 1972

American Pie
The Ziggy Stardust Tour
Puppy Love
Dark Round the Edges
New York Dolls

Page 46 - 1959

Tamla Records
Spitball
The day the music died (Buddy Holly, Ritchie Valens and The Big Bopper (and pilot Roger Petersen} all died.
The Supremes
Robert Smith

Page 47 - 2019

The Cranberries
Billie Eilish
Cats
The Specials
Olivia Newton-John

Page 48 - 1965

Downtown
Maria Callas
The Small Faces
The Doors
Grateful Dead

Page 49 - 2013

Stone Temple Pilots
Set Fire to the Rain and Skyfall
It's the 1000th album to reach No.1 in the chart
Emeli Sandé
Arcade Fire

Page 50 - 1962

Bob Dylan
"Telstar" by the Tornadoes
"Love Me Do" / "P.S. I Love You"
The Mashed Potato
Billy Fury

Page 51 - 1976

Save Your Kisses for Me - Brotherhood of Man
U2
The P-Funk/Rubber Band Earth Tour
New Rose
Bugsy Malone

Page 52 - 1983

New Year's Day
Compact Disc
Dave Mustaine
Pulitzer Price for Music
Moonwalk

Page 53 - 2001

Manic Street Preachers
Gorillaz
Zombies
George Harrison
Hayseed Dixie

Page 54 - 2007

The Best Damn Thing
The Police (Gordon Sumner = Sting)
Madison Square Garden
Amy Winehouse
You could pay what you wanted for the download

Page 55 - 2017

Bananarama (Siobhan Fahey, Sara Dalling and Keren Woodward)
÷
Harry Styles
Stormzy

Sgt. Pepper's Lonely Hearts Club Band
(The Beatles)

Page 56 - 1974

Court and Spark
Rush
Ramones
Abba (Waterloo)
The start of a Portuguese Military Coup
- The "Carnation Revolution"

Page 57 - 1969

A boy named Sue
Lotti Golden
Called the "Amen Break", it features the
most sampled drum beat in music
history.
Blind Faith
In a Silent Way

Page 58 - 1985

Nelson Mandela
3 (Saving all my Love for You,
How will I know, Greatest Love of All)
Wham!
Dire Straits
Live Aid

Page 59 - 1971

The First Glastonbury Festival
My Sweet Lord
Gary Barlow
Jim Morrison
Queen

Page 60 - 2009

Lady Gaga
Inaugural celebration of US President
Barack Obama
Jennifer Hudson
Adele
Crack a Bottle

Page 61 - 1992

To spend more time as a Racing Car
driver
Paul Simon
November Rain
Body Count
Blink-182

Page 62 - 1982

Madonna
Cats
Michael Jackson - Thriller
Under Attack
Eye of the Tiger - Rocky 3

Page 63 - 1999

Lauryn Hill
Diamond
Napster
Christina Aguilera
Coachella

Page 64 - 1978

1. Stayin' Alive / 5. Night Fever
Bowie Knife (Don't try this at home
kids...)
Prince
Dead Kennedys
The Soundhouse Tapes

Page 65 - 1997

Katrina and the Waves
Come to Daddy
Teletubbies
Be Here Now
Phish (Phish Food)

Page 66 - 2003

Cry Baby (by Jemini)
Hurt
Fallen
Beyoncé
Chase & Status

Page 67 - 1990

Bob Marley
$295,000 (Earn a point for $50,000
either way)
Less than a month (married April
27th. File for divorce May 24th)
Pearl Jam
Sinead O'Connor - Nothing
Compares 2 U

Page 68 - 1995

Manic Street Preachers
In Prison. (The album was "Me
Against the World")
Celine Dion
Free as a Bird
Supergrass

Page 69 - 1954

Elvis Costello
Alan Freed
Fender Stratocaster Electric Guitar
Rock around the Clock
That's all right (Mama) or Blue Moon
of Kentucky

Page 70 - 2013

Robin Thicke, Pharrell Williams and T.I.
Babel
Lou Reed
Girls Aloud
Reg Presley

Page 71 - 1968

King Crimson
6540
Kylie Minogue
Frankie Lymon
Hey Jude

Page 72 - 1956

Refrain
John Lennon
Four
Singing the Blues
Ian Curtis

Page 73 - 1982

Kelly Clarkson
MC Dusk
A Little Peace
Come On Eileen
The Model / Computer Love

Page 74 - 1962

Craig and Charlie Reid
Ivor Novello Awards
Joan Baez
Frank Ifield
Four

Page 75 - 1976

Dancing Queen
A Star is Born
Elton John
The Cure
Their Greatest Hits (1971-1975)

Page 76 - 1995

The Ramones
The Corrs
Coolio
The Bends
Poppy

Page 77 - 2005

Scooter
Panic! At the Disco
Confessions on a Dance Floor
Guitar Hero
System of a Down

Page 78 - 1957

John Lennon and Paul McCartney
Keith Levene
All Shook Up
West Side Story
Tom and Jerry

Page 79 - 1980

Radio Caroline
Sony Walkman
Monsters of Rock
John Lennon
Roland TR-808 Drum Machine

Page 80 - 2004

Speakerboxxx/The Love Below
McFly
Back to Bedlam (James Blunt)
Paramore
Gwen Stefani - Love. Angel. Music.
Baby.

Page 81 - 1964

60% (1 point for 10% either way)
The Who
The High Numbers - Zoot Suit / I'm
the Face
The Supremes
Caesar and Cleo

Page 82 - 1993

Oasis
Snoop Dogg
Toni Braxton (self titled debut LP)
Meatloaf
Jamiroquai

Page 83 - 1969

The Woodstock Music and Art

Festival
Dave Grohl
Faces (Formerly Small Faces).
Janis Joplin
The Isle of Wight Festival

Alice Cooper
Grease
Them
Creedence Clearwater Revival
Notorious B.I.G.

Page 84 - 1978

Page 91 - 1987

5 (Kenny Rogers as the Gambler. The Adventure Continues. The Legend Continues. The Luck of the Draw. Playing for Keeps)
15
Mull of Kintyre
Wuthering Heights (Kate Bush)
Billy Idol

The KLF
Kylie Minogue
Bad
$135 million (earn a point for $20 either way..)
Top of the Pops

Page 92 - 1963

Page 85 - 1979

Gary Numan
Heart of Glass
4
Soviet Union
ABC Records

Three (4 if you count "She Loves You" which reached number one twice).
Gerry and the Pacemakers
You'll Never Walk Alone
The audio cassette
Beatlemania

Page 86 - 2009

Page 93 - 1967

Drake
Susan Boyle
Tinchy Stryder
Michael Jackson
Beady Eye

The Doors
Aretha Franklin Day
Pink Floyd - Syd Barrett
Rolling Stone
Otis Redding

Page 87 - 1973

Page 94 - 2003

Tubular Bells by Mike Oldfield
Queen
DJ Kool Herc (Clive Campbell)
AC/DC
Angie

The Thermals
Snow Patrol
50 Cent
Maurice Gibb
Johnny Cash

Page 88 - 1965

Page 95 - 1981

The Supremes
My Generation (The Who)
The 13th Floor Elevators
Jefferson Airplane
(I can't Get No) Satisfaction

Ozzy Osbourne
$20m
Kerrang!
MTV
Bette Davis Eyes

Page 89 - 1992

Page 96 - 1996

Factory Records
MP3
Whitney Houston
R.E.M.
Charli XCX

Jay-Z
Linkin Park
Super Furry Animals
Los Del Rio
Jeffrey Lee Pierce

Page 90 - 1972

Page 97 - 2010

Teddy Pendergrass
Fearless
Justin Bieber
Kickstarts
A-Ha (Lead Singer, Morten Harket)

Page 98 - 2020

Kenny Rogers
He didn't, the contest was cancelled
due to the Covid-19 Pandemic
The Sound of 2020
Conan Gray - The LP debuted at No.5
Little Richard

Page 99 - 1959

Mack the Knife
Juke Box Jury
Ronnie Scott's
Living Doll
Bobby Darin

Page 100 - 1974

Hey Joe
Blondie
Kung Fu Fighting
Victoria Beckham
"Mama" Cass Elliott

Page 101 - 1985

Night Rocker - David Hasselhoff
A-Ha
This is Big Audio Dynamite
Cut the Crap
Tears for Fears

Page 102 - 1971

Carole King
Gypsies, Tramps and Thieves
Elton John
Donna Summer
Eagles

Page 103 - 1989

Phish
Devil's Night Out
Louder than Love. (their 'true' debut on
Indie label SST Records was
"Ultramega OK" in 1988)
Monty Python (Monty Python Sings)
(Terry Gilliam was born in the US)
Like a Prayer

Page 104 - 2012

Boots of Chinese Plastic
Psy, Gangnam Style
Beastie Boys
Buffalo Springfield
Ed Sheeran

Page 105 - 1955

78s
Blackboard Jungle (Bill Haley -
Rock around the Clock)
RCA Victor
Shake, Rattle and Roll
Johnny Cash

Page 106 - 1977

The Clash
Sid Vicious - Sex Pistols
Elvis Presley
The Police
The Specials

Page 107 - 1966

Extreme
Johnny Kidd (and the Pirates)
David Bowie
Eight Miles High
Murray Kaufman (Murray The K).

Page 108 - 1998

A different lead vocalist - Gary
Cherone, not David Lee Roth
Britney Spears
Wide Open Spaces
System of a Down
Judge Dread (Alexander Minto
Hughes)

Page 109 - 1999

Kings of Leon
N.E.R.D.
t.A.T.u. (Lena Katina and Julia
Volkova)
Ednaswap
Dusty Springfield

Page 110 - 2019

Keith Flint
Doris Day
Old Town Road by Lil Nas X
All I Want For Christmas Is You
Someone You Loved

Page 111 - 2014

Pharrell Williams
Frankie Knuckles
Kate Bush
Open the Door to Your Heart (Thought
to be the only copy in existence on the
London record label)
Rudimental, featuring Ella Eyre

Page 112 - 2018

Slayer (the Big Four being Slayer,
Metallica, Megadeth and Anthrax)
Cardi B
Aretha Franklin
BTS (Albums: Love Yourself: Tear, Love
Yourself: Answer, Map of the Soul:
Persona, Map of the Soul: 7)
Taylor Swift (As of 2020 she is now the
most Awarded artist ever, Male or
Female, with 29 Awards)

Page 113 - 1990

Iggy Azalea
The Charlatans
Fine Young Cannibals
One
Portuguese

Page 114 - 2007

OneRepublic
Umbrella
Kanye West - Graduation
Grandmaster Flash and the Furious
Five
Florence and the Machine

Page 115 - 2015

Lemmy (Leader of Motörhead and
vocalist of Hawkwind)
Hello (it was also the first song with
over 1 million digital sales in a week)
James Bay
Muse
Sam Smith

Page 116 - 2002

Fergie
Norah Jones
Scissor Sisters (the single was
"Electrobix")
Avril Lavigne
24 Hour Party People

Page 117 - 2001

Cradle of Filth
The Killers
DJ Tiësto
The Dirt
Aaliyah

Page 118 - 1994

Ten Summoner's Tales
Definitely Maybe
Korn
Iron Maiden
Foo Fighters

Page 119 - 1983

Let's Dance
Mick Jones
Phil Lynott
Quiet Riot
Culture Club

Page 120 - 1960

Scotland
78rpm records
It's now or never
INXS
Paul David Hewson

Page 121 - 1988

The Phantom of the Opera - over
10,000 performances so far
Celine Dion
Nine Inch Nails
Nirvana
Grandmaster Flash and the Furio
Five

Page 122 - 2016

Prince
They're the only two female solo
artists to have Billboard Hot 100
No.1's at over 40 years of age
A Tribe Called Quest (We Got It
From Here... Thank You 4 Your
Service)
Justin Bieber (Love Yourself,
Sorry and What Do You Mean?)
Drake feat. Wizkid & Kyla

Page 123 - 2008

Richey Edwards
Within 2 minutes

Beyoncé
The Dresden Dolls
Leon Jackson - 4th winner of X
Factor/Alexandra Burke - 5th winner
of X Factor

Page 124 - 1984

Judas Priest
Ricky Martin
The Red Hot Chili Peppers
Born in the U.S.A.
Do they know it's Christmas?

Page 125 - 1970

Bridge over Troubled Water
Live at Leeds
Lola (He had to change "Coca-Cola" to
"Cherry Cola" to get airplay in the UK).
The Isle of Wight Festival
Derek and the Dominos

Page 126 - 2000

Overload
Coldplay
Madonna
NSYNC
Ian Dury

Page 127 - 1958

Have "Twangy" guitar will travel
Jerry Lee Lewis
Ricky Nelson with Poor Little Fool
Vic Damone
Paul Weller

Page 128 - 2011

Little Mix
Plan B
Born This Way
Michael Bublé
Album - 21. Single - Someone Like You

Page 129 - 1986

The Smiths
Pet Shop Boys
Sub Pop
Salt-N-Pepper
Guns N' Roses

Page 130 - 2006

Mary J. Blige (Be Without You)
Hey Joe

Lordi (Hard Rock Hallelujah)
Taylor Swift
Top of the Pops

Page 131 - 1975

Bohemian Rhapsody - Queen
Will.I.Am
Slade in Flame
Jive Talkin'
Sex Pistols

Page 132 - 1997

Missy Elliot
MMMBop - Hanson
Two posthumous No.1 singles
Bittersweet Symphony
Come on Over

Page 133 - 1961

Wooden Heart
Blue Moon, Moon River
Johnny Remember Me
The Boll Weevil Song
The Beach Boys

Page 134 - 2017

Chance the Rapper. He won Best
New Artist, Best Rap Performance
and Best Rap Album
Chris Cornell
Glen Campbell
Chester Bennington
Chuck Berry

Printed in Great Britain
by Amazon

84715674R00086